D0213075

*Thomas Traherne*

Twayne's English Authors Series

Arthur F. Kinney, Editor

*University of Massachusetts, Amherst*

TEAS 342

# *Thomas Traherne*

## By Malcolm M. Day

*Indiana University of Pennsylvania*

*Twayne Publishers • Boston*

PR
3736
.T7
.D3

*Thomas Traherne*

Malcolm M. Day

Copyright © 1982
Twayne Publishers
A Division of G. K. Hall & Company
70 Lincoln Street
Boston, Massachusetts 02111

Book Production by Marne B. Sultz

Book Design by Barbara Anderson

Printed on permanent/durable acid-free
paper and bound in the United States of
America.

**Library of Congress Cataloging in
Publication Data**

Day, Malcolm M.
    Thomas Traherne.

(Twayne's English authors series ; TEAS
342)
Bibliography: p. 168
Includes index.
    1. Traherne, Thomas, d.
1674—Criticism and
interpretation.   I. Title.   II. Series.
PR3736.T7Z64     821'.4   81-6728
ISBN 0-8057-6742-8        AACR2

## Editor's Note

Thomas Traherne's work, much of it not understood until recent times, nevertheless lays strong claim to our attention among the achievements of seventeenth-century English writers of religious poetry and prose. In this new general study of Traherne's accomplishment, Malcolm Day argues that, even without much biographical information, the intentions and meanings of his work are clearly set forth by the way they are structured. What emerges is a Traherne as much teacher as contemplative or poet, a man "both admirably sane and prophetic" whose mysticism was not essentially affective or contemplative but ideological and speculative. His work, Day contends, conveys direct, ingenuous, joyful impressions, yet it consistently illustrates how Traherne "saw the whole range of human life and Christian progress toward ultimate Felicity, not in the concrete experiences of a particular person striving for God, but of a set of ideas, thoughts to be comprehended by the Soul, intellections by which we put our minds in frame." The "erosion" of time and space, the blurring of traditional observations and categories of thought, thus emerges as only one of Traherne's techniques of instructing his readers. Day's study is a continuation of the current interest in Traherne, concentrating on Traherne's use of abstraction, paradox, and repetition to entice the mind to a sight of infinity and eternity as they are not only in childlike vision but in their fundamental nature—to see but also to be "in-formed" by the "Naked Truth."

—Arthur F. Kinney

# Contents

## About the Author

Malcolm M. Day is Professor of English at Indiana University of Pennsylvania, where he has taught since 1970, serving for a year as Director of Graduate Studies. He received his B.A. and M.A. degrees from the University of Florida and his Ph.D. from Western Reserve University in Cleveland. He has taught at Indiana University at South Bend and was a Danforth Fellow in 1960 and a research fellow at the Newberry Library in Chicago in 1967. One of Professor Day's major interests is the mystical writers of the seventeenth century, and he has published papers on this subject in the *Hanover Forum* as well as articles on Traherne in *Studies in Philology*.

# Preface

The increasing interest in Thomas Traherne's prose and poetry over the last twenty years has been stimulated by more than H. M. Margoliouth's scholarly edition of 1958. As the dogmatic certainties of modern Western thought—whether of a scientific, philosophic, or religious sort—have come to be questioned by various nonmaterialist modes of thinking arising in part from modern physics and from ancient Eastern traditions, the writings of Traherne have begun to seem less naive than they were once thought to be. Recent critics have recognized that Traherne has something more to offer than fantastic speculations about time and eternity or the infinite powers of the soul. Thus, an early tendency to see Traherne as a charming child who insisted upon singing his lovely but meaningless Neoplatonic songs (as Sir Arthur Quiller-Couch implied in *Felicities of Thomas Traherne* [London: P. J. and A. E. Dobell, 1934]) has been changing in the last few years to an attitude of greater respect, as the genuinely profound nature of his thought has been more fully revealed.

The present study reflects this changing attitude by taking Traherne's thinking seriously and accepting its highly metaphysical character as necessarily paradoxical and symbolic, having the same basic character as the thought of such earlier mystics as Meister Eckhart and Nicholas of Cusa and of such traditionalists as Frithjof Schuon and Ananda Coomaraswamy in our own day. Although Traherne expressed his ideas in the language of Christianity, his thinking was dominated by the concept that ultimate reality consists of the eternal ideas of all things existing infinitely and simultaneously in the Mind of God, and this concept is the single most significant influence upon the basically meditative structures of his work as well as upon that paralleling, repetitive rhetoric which he developed and used with great skill to express his deepest beliefs. Such rhetoric is also imitative of biblical poetry; it cannot be confined to a regular metrical line or rhyme scheme, and because it is not compatible with such regularity it tends to damage Traherne's efforts at conventional verse.

This study also sees Traherne as a part of the Restoration period in which he lived: a thinker who returned to an earlier Neoplatonic metaphysic and did so boldly, with a trust in its reasonableness and its compatibility with Christianity that others in his period were also assuming; but although Traherne's trust in reason did take him outside the ecclesiastical institution into the open air, it never took him so far as to make him forget the uncontrollable mystery on the bestial floor. Always, at the heart of Traherne's thinking lay the wondrous miracle of the "incarnation" of the One in (and into) the many of time and space.

This study, finally, deals with all the published works of Traherne as well as the yet-unpublished "Select Meditations." It does not discuss the four other unpublished manuscripts because only the Traherne specialist is likely to read them and because they have been excellently and fully discussed in a number of scholarly articles by Carol Marks [Sicherman] to which the interested reader is urged to turn.

Although many people have been of great help over the years in which I have been writing this study, I shall not attempt to name them for fear of leaving out some who should have been included. I owe, as always, my deepest debt to Charlotte, Jonathan, Geoffrey, Gary, and Andrea, who merely endured.

Malcolm M. Day

Indiana University of Pennsylvania

# Acknowledgments

Grateful acknowledgment is made to the following publishers of Traherne's works:

Oxford University Press for permission to quote from *Traherne: Centuries, Poems, and Thanksgivings* (1958), 2 vols., ed. H. M. Margoliouth and from *Thomas Traherne: Poems, Centuries and Three Thanksgivings* (1966), ed. Anne Ridler, also for permission to quote from Douglas Bush, *English Literature in the Earlier Seventeenth Century,* (2d ed. 1962).

Cornell University Press, for permission to quote from Traherne's *Christian Ethicks* (1968), ed., Carol Marks and George Guffey.

Cooper Square Publishers for permission to quote from *The Poetical Works of Thomas Traherne* (1932), ed., Gladys Wade.

Passages from Arnold Williams, *The Common Expositor: An Account of the Commentaries on Genesis, 1527–1633* (1948) are reprinted by permission of the University of North Carolina Press.

Passages from Douglas Jordan, *The Temple of Eternity* (1972) are reprinted by permission of Kennikat Press.

Passages from *The Paradise Within* (1964), by Louis Martz are reprinted by permission of Yale University Press.

Quotations from *Walt Whitman Handbook* (1946) by Gay Wilson Allen are printed by permission of Hendricks House.

Passages from G. R. Cragg, *From Puritanism to the Age of Reason* (1950) and from C. S. Lewis, *The Discarded Image* (1970) are reprinted by permission of Cambridge University Press.

Passages from Helen White, Ruth Wallerstein, and Ricardo Quintana, *Seventeenth-Century Verse and Prose,* 2 vols. (1952) are reprinted by permission of Macmillan Publishing Co.

Quotations from Stanley Stewart, *The Expanded Voice* (1970) are printed with permission of the Henry E. Huntington Library and Art Gallery.

Passages from Ernst Cassirer, *The Platonic Renaissance in England* (1953), translated by James P. Pettegrove are reprinted by permission of the University of Texas Press.

Emma Gurney Salter's translation of Nicholas of Cusa's *The Vision of God* (1928) is cited by permisson of Elsevier-Dutton Publishing Co.

Special thanks are due to Louis L. Martz for permission to quote freely from Traherne's "Select Meditations" (Osborn Collection, Yale University).

# Chronology

1637    Thomas Traherne born in Hereford, shortly before October 20, the son of a shoemaker, very likely related to a family of Trahernes in nearby Lugwardine as well as to an elder Philip Traherne, twice mayor of Hereford.

1640–1645    Thomas may have been placed under the care of the elder Philip Traherne, who provided for the education of Thomas and his brother Philip.

1652    Entered Brasenose College, Oxford, as a Commoner, March 1.

1656    Received Bachelor of Arts from Brasenose, October 13. Began entries in "Early Notebook," making last entry in 1660.

1657    Presented to the living of Credenhill, about five miles from Hereford, December 30, by the Commissioners for Approbation of Public Preachers under the Commonwealth and by the presentation of the Countess Dowager of Kent. Did not begin residency at this time but held the position until his death.

1660    Ordained under the Restoration as deacon and priest, October 20.

1661    Made Master of Arts at Brasenose by decree, November 6, and reappointed at Credenhill under new sponsors. May have returned to Oxford for study toward Bachelor of Divinity degree.

1662–1663    Probably wrote "Select Meditations" and perhaps began serious composition of poetry.

1664    May have returned from Oxford and begun first residence at Credenhill.

| | |
|---|---|
| 1666–1668 | Engaged in close study of Marsilio Ficino's commentary on Plato, copying extracts in Latin into the "Ficino Notebook." Perhaps wrote most of the *Centuries of Meditations*. |
| 1669 | Received Bachelor of Divinity from Brasenose, December 11. Left Credenhill and moved to London as domestic chaplain to Sir Orlando Bridgeman, then Lord Keeper of the Great Seal, with whom he spent the remaining years of his life. |
| 1670 | Began intense literary activity. May have finished the *Centuries of Meditations* and collected and arranged his poems in the Dobell manuscript. Wrote the "Church's Year-Book" (between April and November 1670) and probably *Meditations on the Six Days of the Creation* as well as most of the *Thanksgivings* in the same or following year. Began making entries in his "Commonplace Book," used in part as notes for *Christian Ethicks*. |
| 1672 | Moved to Teddington, Bridgeman's family seat, where he continued as Bridgeman's chaplain and as minister of Teddington Church. Visited Credenhill and spent some time at Oxford doing research for and writing *Roman Forgeries*. May also have written the final Thanksgiving (for the Nation). |
| 1673 | *Roman Forgeries* published anonymously. |
| 1674 | Traherne died in the first week of October and was buried under the reading-desk at Teddington Church on October 10. |
| 1675 | *Christian Ethicks* published. |
| 1677 | Five small houses owned by Thomas given to the mayor and parish of All Saints, Hereford, by Philip, in accordance with Thomas's earlier expressed wishes. |
| 1699 | *Thanksgivings* published anonymously by the Reverend George Hickes as *A Serious and Pathetical Contemplation of the Mercies of God, in Several most Devout and Sublime Thanksgivings for the same.* |

1717   *Meditations on the Six Days of the Creation* published by Nathaniel Spinckes as the first part of *A Collection of Meditations and Devotions* attributed to Mrs. Susanna Hopton.

1895   *Centuries of Meditations* and the Dobell folio of poems discovered on a London bookstall by W. T. Brooke.

1903   First publication of the Dobell sequence of poems, by Bertram Dobell.

1908   First publication of the *Centuries,* by Dobell.

1910   The Burney sequence of poems published as *Poems of Felicity.*

1958   Definitive edition of Traherne's *Centuries, Poems and Thanksgivings* by H. M. Margoliouth.

1964   Manuscript of "Select Meditations" discovered by James Osborn.

# Chapter One

# A Spokesman for Felicity

## A Short Life

Over the last fifteen to twenty years we have learned a few new facts about Thomas Traherne's (1637–1674) life, but we still have so little positive information that only the broadest generalizations can be made concerning his biography and its relation to what he wrote. H. M. Margoliouth in his definitive edition of Traherne (1958) published all the information then known, and except for some details concerning Traherne's Credenhill residency and some matters of mistaken attribution and chronology, there is not much to change in his account.[1] We do know enough, however, to get some idea of Traherne's character and personality, and with an understanding of the relevant historical, intellectual conditions in which he lived we can at least be prepared to read him intelligently.

Margoliouth has established beyond reasonable doubt that Traherne "was born in 1637, before but perhaps not long before 20 October."[2] There is still some uncertainty about his specific birthplace, but Traherne was probably born in Hereford, near the Welsh border, and was related to some well-to-do Trahernes in Lugwardine, two or three miles to the northeast. It has been generally assumed, primarily on the basis of the statements of both Anthony à Wood and John Aubrey (who probably shared his information with Wood), that Traherne was the son of a shoemaker.[3] That he was able to attend Oxford and become highly educated suggests that the further speculations concerning his receiving help from an elder Philip Traherne (1566–1645), twice mayor of Hereford, could also have some merit.

He entered Brasenose College, Oxford, on March 1, 1652, having probably experienced some of the sufferings of the Civil Wars which touched royalist Hereford on three separate occasions before Traherne was eight years old. He received a B.A. from Oxford on October 13,

1656, and may have, as Wood says, "left the house [Oxford] for a time [and] entred into the sacred function." All we know for certain is what records in the Lambeth Palace Library tell us, that he was admitted the following year, on December 30, 1657, under regulations established by the Commonwealth "to the Rectory of Crednell, alias Creddenhill, Co. Hereford,"[4] a small parish about five miles from the great cathedral city.

It is possible that this rectorship was awarded to Traherne to further his education, for there is no evidence that he took up residence at Credenhill in 1657. We do know he was ordained deacon and priest on October 20, 1660, under the Restoration. And the next positive fact we have is that Brasenose awarded him an M.A. by decree on November 6, 1661. During the five years from his first degree (1656) to his second one in 1661 it seems likely that he was spending most of his time studying at Oxford rather than performing parish duties at Credenhill—he would have been only twenty in 1657—and Margoliouth argues that such was the case, asserting that Traherne did not take up residency in his parish until after he had received the M.A.[5] There is some reason to think, however, that Traherne may not have begun his duties at Credenhill even then, and it was not until 1664 that he finally settled in at the parish to which he had been presented earlier by the Commonwealth Commissioners and (in 1661) also by the bishops of the newly reestablished church.[6]

It is probable, as Margoliouth believes, that the granting of Traherne's B.D. in 1669 and his becoming the chaplain to Sir Orlando Bridgeman, then Keeper of the Great Seal, are related events, but it is not clear what set of relationships or other events led to Bridgeman's coming to know Traherne. Both shared the same general platonic mode of thinking (Traherne's predecessor was Hezekiah Burton, a Cambridge Platonist), and the speculation that their acquaintance came about through the good offices of Traherne's close friend, Mrs. Susanna Hopton (1627–1709), who was also the aunt of his brother Philip's wife, has at least circumstantial evidence to support it.[7] The possible connections Mrs. Hopton might have had with Traherne's appointment are complex, but in their simplest form they involve, on the one hand, the possibility that Susanna Hopton (née Harvey) and the wife (also a Harvey) of Heneage Finch (1621–1682), solicitor-General under

Charles II, were relatives. On another hand, they involve the certainty that Philip Traherne was indebted to and acquainted with Heneage Finch at some time in his life and that Finch and Bridgeman were close friends. A further interesting fact is that Finch's younger half-sister was the Lady Anne Conway, with whom the well-known Cambridge Platonist Henry More (1614–1687) carried on a long personal and intellectual friendship;[8] but all these possible and/or actual relationships do not tell us exactly how Bridgeman learned of Traherne and came to appoint him chaplain. They do, however, indicate that Traherne was no simple, unsophisticated child from a backward village in West England warbling his mystical wood notes. He was, rather, a highly educated man of some genuine social status and real promise in the intellectual world of his day.[9]

With Bridgeman and his family Traherne found a congenial situation that stimulated in him an intense activity of composition. We now are nearly certain that almost every extant work of Traherne's (the exceptions are the "Early Notebook," "Select Meditations," the "Ficino Notebook," and an unknown number of poems), published or unpublished, was written within the five years between his moving to London and his death in 1674. Traherne must have worked extremely hard, for even though several of the items are either revisions of the work of others or notes and comments upon other books, they represent altogether a considerable amount of material for anyone to have produced in so short a time. But since most of the material was lost for over three hundred years, Traherne was soon forgotten almost completely except by his brother Philip and Mrs. Hopton, both of whom evidently planned at separate times to have certain of his manuscripts published. Mrs. Hopton was successful in having at least the *Thanksgivings* published in 1699, but Philip's editing of the poems lay anonymously in manuscript until the beginning of our own century.

Thomas saw *Roman Forgeries* through the press, but he did not see *Christian Ethicks* published. Bridgeman became ill and died in late June of 1674, and Thomas Traherne himself died in the first week of October, being buried on the tenth of the month under the lectern in the church at Teddington, Middlesex, where Bridgeman had taken his household after his removal from the King's service. A contemporary (perhaps Mrs. Hopton) wrote of Traherne's personality:

He was a man of a cheerful and sprightly Temper, free from any thing of the sourness or formality, by which some great pretenders of Piety rather disparage and misrepresent true Religion, than recommend it; and therefore was very affable and pleasant in his Conversation, ready to do all good Offices to his Friends, and Charitable to the Poor almost beyond his ability. But being removed out of the Country to the service of the late Lord Keeper *Bridgman,* as his Chaplain, he died young, and got early to those blissful Mansions, to which he at all times aspir'd.[10]

That he was a generally cheerful, sociable, and seriously religious person is the impression given by everything he wrote (though *Roman Forgeries* shows that he could be bitingly ironic), and something of the same cheerful, generous character is hinted at in a letter to William Thomas, Dean of Worcester, written by Thomas Good (Master of Balliol College and formerly of Hereford). It is a poignant note which at least suggests that a life of considerable potential had ended before its possibilities could come close to being realized: "I believe it is not news to you that Tom Traherne is dead, one of the most pious ingenious men that ever I was acquainted with."[11]

## The Nature of Traherne's Thought

If one were asked to characterize Traherne's fundamental outlook on life with a single word, he would almost certainly choose "joy." Almost every page of Traherne's best known work urges the reader to enjoy the world, and, as one reads, he too may begin to feel that the world is overflowing with the blessings of God. If we do not enjoy the world, insists Traherne, we not only destroy our own happiness but also the very purpose for which the world was made. The world is glorious, and we must learn to recognize it as such:

Your Enjoyment of the World is never right, till evry Morning you awake in Heaven: see your self in your fathers Palace: and look upon the Skies and the Earth and the Air, as Celestial Joys: having such a Reverend Esteem of all, as if you were among the Angels. (*CM* 1.28)[12]

No doubt if most of us could view the sky, the earth, and the air with the intensity of esteem and respect Traherne recommends, we would be much happier than we are. But it is difficult for us to believe as thoroughly as Traherne does that the world is good or that man is capable of such positive response to it, and for this reason some have tended to dismiss Traherne as an immature optimist, too superficial to be taken seriously. Such an evaluation has been made only too often by scholars in the past, and it is still sometimes repeated. For example, Douglas Bush has said that "neither as Christian nor as philosopher does Traherne seem quite mature,"[13] and one of our ablest Traherne scholars has recently expressed a like lament for the shallowness of Traherne's Christian philosophy. In a comment upon several passages from Traherne's "Church's Year-Book" Carol Marks writes:

There is a certain naiveté about all this; it is too simple. All we need do is love "Simple, Naked Souls," recognize the true worth of things, and all will be well . . . . In the end, that simplicity diminishes our faith in Traherne's sincere but facile professions of practicality. His conviction of man's goodness can inspire us to admiration, perhaps to envy, but not to assent. Opposed in his own day by the theology of Original Sin, Traherne's joyful optimism crashes today against the Berlin wall, the Vietnamese war.[14]

But Traherne's optimism only appears to be simple and naive; it is a profoundly realistic and mature view that does not depend upon man's good behavior for its acceptability, nor does the presence of human suffering invalidate it. Because Traherne's vision is cosmic, perceiving all temporal events in the light of eternity, it can encompass all the Berlin walls and Vietnamese (or Trojan) wars throughout history without making light of their meaning as occasions for human agony nor denying their existence as a contradiction of its perspective. It is not the relative and temporal human position from which Traherne's optimism arises but the infinite and eternal perspective of the divine Being—of which man and his cosmos are a manifestation—that fills him with joy and wonder. What Traherne celebrates at all times is the miracle of Creation, the presence of the divine substance in and behind all existence—and that eternal drama is good because the divine substance is good, even though the Crucifixion is an inevitable and fundamental part of that drama. Traherne's particular significance as a Christian Neoplatonist and mystic is that he sees into this mystery of the foundations of existence and tries to teach others that if they, too, learn to see it, all things will appear wonderful and miraculous because they are the manifestations of God. Because they are also relative phenomena, however, their true divine nature cannot be perceived directly by one's bodily eyes, and they are necessarily limited and imperfect in themselves even though their ultimate nature is divine and perfect:

they who are angry with the Deity for not shewing Himself to their Bodily Eys are not displeased with that maner of Revelation, but that He is such a God as He is . . . . What Perfections then would they hav that Body to Express? If His Infinity, that Body then must be infinit. Upon which the same Absurdity would follow as before. for being infinit it would exclude all Being beside out of Place. (*CM* II.20)

Thus, to see the world as both imperfect in itself and yet perfect insofar as it is a manifestation of the divine Being, requires spiritual perception, and this is not available to those who cannot grasp the world or themselves from the standpoint of eternity.

Traherne will, then, seem immature and naive to those whose perspective is confined to the temporal condition, and because few can transcend the personal, temporal perspective in order to perceive things in this spiritual way, they tend to respond more positively to writers who reflect a consciousness of life's imperfections and difficulties. Thus, aside from preferring the poetry of such men as John Donne, George Herbert, Richard Crashaw, Andrew Marvell, and Henry Vaughn because it is better poetry, many tend to judge the poets themselves as also more mature than Traherne because these writers "recognize" the darkness in man's life and speak of man's weaknesses and sins. Even Vaughn, who of the metaphysical poets most resembles Traherne, never forgets the "difference" between man and God, this world and the next:

But living where the Sun
Doth all things wake, and where all mix and tyre
Themselves and others, I consent and run
        To ev'ry myre,
    And by this world's ill-guiding light,
    Erre more then I can do my night.

                                                    ("The Night")[15]

Traherne, typically, is full of joy and light and the "impersonal" principles by which the cosmos is to be "appreciated" and the soul made one with God:

You shall be Glorified, you shall liv in Communion with Him, you shall
ascend into the Throne of the Highest Heavens; . . . you shall be Like Him,
when you enjoy the World as He doth. (*CM* II.18)

But Traherne's optimism is founded upon the highest spiritual awareness, and it should not be identified with the shallower, deistic form
that was developing in the Restoration intellectual climate, to which it
owes only its general outward character and impetus.

As the century moved toward the Augustan Age, a general increase
in optimism was obviously taking place. The younger religious writers
(those born after 1630) were all less inclined to emphasize the world's
darkness or man's precarious state. With the rapidly increasing acceptance of empirical reason as the means of obtaining truth, it was
becoming easier to accept a fundamentally rational view of the universe,
and in outward temperament and attitude Traherne has much in
common with such Restoration contemporaries as Joseph Glanvill
(1636–1680), Robert South (1634–1716), Isaac Barrow (1630–1677),
and Edward Stillingfleet (1635–1699).[16] As a contemporary of these
men, Traherne was affected similarly by the same general climate of
attitudes and events. The bloodshed of the Civil Wars and the fierce
conflicts between Presbyterians, Independents, and sectarians of every
kind influenced a growing desire among later writers to find some
means of establishing a more tolerant and stable intellectual condition.
Glanvill, for example, who was a fellow student of Traherne's at
Oxford, wrote *The Vanity of Dogmatizing* (1661) in order to encourage
men to reflect upon the relative uncertainty of knowledge and, while
asserting their opinions, to admit that they could be mistaken:

True knowledge is modest and wary, 'tis ignorance that is so bold, and
presuming . . . *Confidence in Opinions* evermore dwells with untamed
*passions,* and is maintain'd upon the depraved *obstinacy* of an ungovern'd
*spirit. . . .* To be *confident* in *Opinions* is ill *manners,* and *immodesty.*[17]

Glanvill did not mean that knowledge was inevitably uncertain. In
fact, his mild skepticism was the kind necessary to true scientific
inquiry, which must assume that "Confidence *in uncertainties, is the
greatest enemy to what is certain.*"As he says, he has *"no design against*
Science: [his] indeavor is to promote it."[18]

Stillingfleet echoed this same tone of reasonableness where religion
was concerned:

In Matters of Truth and Religion, Reason and Evidence ought to sway Men, and not Passion and Noise; and though Men cannot command their Judgments, they may and ought to do their Expressions.[19]

Similarly, both South, who was Public Orator at Oxford from 1660 to 1667, and Barrow, a prominent preacher whom Traherne read, wrote with a tone of detached and careful reasoning. What G. R. Cragg has assured us of the later Restoration was certainly in evidence earlier than 1660:

The whole temper of the times was hostile to the old forms of dogmatic certainty. People were tired of extremes of every kind. They had grown weary of the fierce intolerance with which their fathers had fought about many things.[20]

Thus, in Traherne's early years a trust in the rational faculty was already leading toward a more tolerant approach to problems and a growing tendency to reduce conflict by an "emphasis on God's benevolence and man's participation in the joy which motivates and accompanies such benevolence."[21] John Tillotson (1630–1694), whom Cragg called "almost a symbol of the later Restoration period," was, in fact, convinced that the goodness of God was so fundamental a principle that no proposition could deny it, whether that proposition was asserted by an angel or by Calvin himself:

If an Apostle, or an angel from heaven teach any doctrine which plainly overthrows the goodness and justice of God, let him be accursed. For every man hath greater assurance that God is good and just than he can have of any subtle speculations about predestination and the decrees of God.[22]

This assurance of the goodness of God was a strong influence in Traherne's lifetime, and it was related to and supported by an equally strong assurance that reason was the only valid tool for discovering truth. The leading intellectuals and preachers of the age recommended, in fact, an application of reason to religion that resembled the method of new science, and although their thinking carried the seeds of a sterile deism, at its inception it insisted that God must be more than a celestial mechanic and that His nature must conform to our deepest feelings of justice and righteousness, our common sense of decency and moral law.[23] In his own trust in reason and God's goodness Traherne is obviously conforming to the same general pattern of thinking engaged in by other men of the Restoration. "I was Guided by an Implicit Faith in Gods Goodness" (*CM* III.53), Traherne says in explanation of how he arrived at the doctrines of his faith, but these doctrines were ultimately founded upon the great ideas of Christian Neoplatonism and mysticism, not upon a simpler rationalism like that of later deists.

## Traherne and Cambridge Platonism

Traherne's view of reason thus differs from the view of the major Restoration preachers, for, as time went on, these later Latitudinarians, as they were sometimes called, saw reason in an increasingly empirical light, much like the Baconian and Hobbesian tool for arriving at correct conclusions on the basis of factual evidence. The seventeenth century had inherited a concept of the rational faculty that included, as its highest part, the power of seeing Truth directly, without the need of an inductive process; this *intellectus* was traditionally considered man's most godlike power and, as C. S. Lewis explains, could perform "the simple (i.e., indivisible, uncompounded) grasp of an intelligible truth," in contradistinction to *reasoning,* which Lewis says was "the progression towards an intelligible truth by going from one understood . . . point to another."[24] Such a concept of intuitive reason outwardly resembles the Stoic belief in a discernible, natural, moral law, and the two were blended in the commonplace term, Right Reason.[25] As most seventeenth-century men used it, Right Reason was an intuitive power intimately related to God, and although it was capable of following a true inductive process, it was also the means of grasping intelligible truth. It is in the greater intensity of Traherne's emphasis upon this relation of Right Reason to God's own mind that he differs from the later Latitudinarians such as Glanvill, Stillingfleet, and other Restoration preachers, and finds closer philosophical allies among the Cambridge Platonists.

It was this earlier group of men—Benjamin Whichcote (1609–1683), Ralph Cudworth (1617–1688), John Smith (1618–1652), and Henry More—who had provided the major intellectual environment for the Restoration, but as Cragg has pointed out, a certain spiritual intensity of the Cambridge men was for the most part lost by those who came after them:

Burnet has assured us that the main influence in molding the thought of the Latitudinarians was the teaching and example of the Cambridge Platonists. At many points this influence can be traced in the mature writings of the younger group of men. They emphasize reason and exalt morality, but the differences between them are as important as the similarities. There is a vein of genius in the Cambridge Platonists which their able but pedestrian successors lack. In Smith and Whichcote there is a depth which is missing in Patrick and Stillingfleet. You can transmit a certain kind of rationalism, but mysticism is a subtler and more elusive matter. Something of incalculable value had faded into the light of common day.[26]

This "something of incalculable value" is a matter of the strength with which Right Reason is believed to be a real function of God Himself. The Cambridge philosophers were deeply concerned about the potential threat to spirituality posed by the advance of the new mechanical philosophy, and to counteract it they emphasized the spiritual nature of Right Reason, claiming that it had the ability to know both God's moral law and the laws of the physical universe. As Ernst Cassirer has said:

To scientific induction, as set forth by Bacon, they [the Cambridge Platonists] oppose the rights of moral and religious experience. Such experience is neglected and debased, if, as does empiricism, one recognizes experience only in the form of sense-perception and considers it as valid only in this form. There is experience not only of the sensible and the corporal, but also of the spiritual and intellectual; not only of the physical, but also of the intelligible.[27]

And because reason in man is, in the language of Proverbs 20:27, "The Candle of the Lord," it is impossible for reason (if functioning properly) to contradict faith. The Cambridge Platonists asserted such an impossibility with tireless repetition. Nathanael Culverwell (1618–1651), for one, challenged his opponents to "Name but the time . . . when ever right Reason did oppose one jot or apex of the Word of God."[28] And Whichcote, the real father of Cambridge Platonism,

pointed out numerous times that "True *Reason* is so far from being an
Enemy to any matter of Faith; that a man is disposed and qualified by
Reason, for the entertaining those matters of Faith that are proposed by
God."[29] The men who followed the Cambridge Platonists also understood the virtual identity between reason and the mind of God, and
Glanvill made a memorable statement of it: *"Reason* and *Faith* are at
perfect Unisons: the disharmony is in the *Phancy* . . . *Reason* being the
Image of the Creators Wisdom copied out in the Creature."[30] But as
time passed, Glanvill and the Restoration Latitudinarians began to see
reason's true character more in its ability to resolve whatever problems
it undertook than in its ability to know spiritual truth by direct
intuition.

In the Cambridge Platonists, however, a tendency to weigh all
propositions in the scale of reason could and did exist simultaneously
with a passionate spiritual exaltation and an absorbing devotion to
holiness. In the later century the "Candle of the Lord" perhaps came too
closely to resemble a Bunsen burner, but for the Cambridge men (and
for Traherne even more clearly than for most) reason still existed in
genuine equipoise with mystical fervor. As a result the Cambridge
Platonists steered a narrow course between mechanism and enthusiasm,
condemning what Henry More calls a "vulgar fanatical Enthusiasm" as
thoroughly as Thomas Hobbes or any other mechanistic philosopher,
while also praising a "true and warrantable Enthusiasm." In his *Enthusiasmus Triumphatus* (1656), where he "followed," as Glanvill said,
*"Enthusiastick effects* to their proper Origine,"[31] More asserts that a
fervent faith and joy are the natural result of the soul's love of God and
that they are open to every soul:

Not one word has all this time been spoken against that true and warrantable
Enthusiasm, of devout and holy Souls, who are so strangely transported in
that vehement Love they bear towards God, and that unexpressible Joy and
Peace they find in him . . . To such Enthusiasm as this, which is but the
triumph of the Soul of man inebriated, as it were, with the delicious sense of
the divine life, that blessed Root and Original of all holy wisdom and virtue,
I must declare my self as much a friend, as I am to the vulgar fanatical
Enthusiasm a professed enemy.[32]

It is likely, then, that Traherne's trust in the preeminence of the
intuitive reason (*intellectus* or Right Reason) came to him chiefly from

the Cambridge Platonists, but his education at Oxford must have been a strong influence upon his acceptance of the power of a more "natural," empirical reason. Contrary to what has sometimes been assumed, Traherne's education at Oxford was not simply conservative or backward looking. It is true that officially both Oxford and Cambridge maintained a primarily traditional curriculum, but learning did not consist merely of such official staples as "scholastic ethics, Ramist geometry, and. . . history as written in the third century A.D.,"[33] nor was it only a matter of scholastic training in such techniques of logic and debate as lecture, disputation, and declamation.[34] Scholars were also made aware of contemporary scientific, philosophic, and practical issues. Tutors encouraged their students to read modern works and to engage in the free research of library holdings. Under the influence of John Wilkins (1614–1672), Master of Wadham College from 1648 to 1659, Oxford became, in fact, *"the* center of scientific studies in the 1650's,"[35] and it was the earliest meeting place of a group that later became instrumental in founding the Royal Society. Although Traherne was at Brasenose, he could hardly have been isolated from the activities of other colleges, and he was familiar with Baconian science as well as physics, astronomy, and anatomy.

Traherne, in fact, could have studied under William Petty (1623–1687), professor of anatomy at Brasenose, an economist, and a famous scientist who was chiefly responsible for the fabulous "raising" of the corpse of the unjustly hanged Anne Greene. He must also have either known or known about such men as Christopher Wren (1632–1723), John Wallis (1616–1703), and Robert Boyle (1627–1691), all of whom were attracted to Oxford by Wilkins. He would certainly have heard about their work in anatomy, astronomy, and chemistry, and must have been aware of the fact that they were carrying on experiments with various "mechanical devices, ranging from dials and flying machines to beehives."[36] The spirit of free inquiry and association that these men enjoyed at Oxford, virtually unhampered by the problems of religious or political differences, was stimulated by the new scientific need for objectivity and careful procedure, and that need was also helping to create an atmosphere of toleration and compromise toward opposing viewpoints among intelligent, practical men at Oxford as well as outside of it:

Science provided a respite, a non-controversial topic of conversation and joint endeavor, in which men of varying religious and political views might have "the satisfaction of breathing a freer air, and of conversing in quiet one with another, without being engaged in the passions and madness of that dismal Age."[37]

Traherne was not one of the virtuosi, but at Oxford he must certainly have absorbed something of the tolerant and rational spirit of inquiry under which scientists were working at the university. Not only did he respond positively to the new vastness of the Copernican universe but, interestingly enough, he also seemed to see the material world as, without God, dead and void of meaning. In his own words about his education he accepts knowledge of nature as good in itself although he insists that this knowledge must be viewed in the light of its ethical significance:

He that Knows the Secrets of Nature with Albertus Magnus, or the Motions of the Heavens with Galilao, or . . . of whatever els with the greatest Artist; He is nothing. if he Knows them meerly for Talk or idle Speculation, or Transeunt and External Use. But He that Knows them for Valu, and Knows them His own: shall Profit infinitly. (*CM* III.41)

In spite of the somewhat conservative nature of Oxford's official curriculum, Traherne was educated in an environment that encouraged a trust in reason and a use of it in one's approach to the world. By the time he entered his life as a clergyman he had absorbed both sides of the current double perspective on reason, and like the earlier Cambridge Platonists he accepted the naturalness of the reasoning process as a genuine path to truth. But Traherne also balanced reason's involvement with the physical world against its equally genuine concern with the intuitive perception of spiritual things and blended them in such a way that reason's contemplation of nature was to reveal, not simply "the order of things as they have been disposed by God,"[38] but the very being of God Himself within that "order of things," and that is an important distinction.[39] It is thus a "proper" vision of the world that prepares the soul for union with God more even than the offices of church and priest. The glass of nature becomes the means by which the soul can focus the candle of the Lord and make it burn brightly enough to light one's way through the darkest night. In a unique way, then, for Traherne: *"Faith* is by *Reason* confirmed, and Reason is by Faith perfected" (*CE,* 112).[40]


## Traherne and Mystical Tradition

Although it may not seem so, Traherne's trust in both a natural and a supernatural reason does not remove him from the mystical tradition. If, on one side, reason is able to perceive spiritual things, then it can come to know God and expect to become one with Him. The intuitive power of *intellectus* can certainly be interpreted as a mystical concept which, because it involves seeing directly what is spiritually meaningful, supports the idea that the soul can thereby be united with God. The Cambridge Platonists believed in and discussed the deification of the soul, and Traherne makes the idea virtually the cornerstone of his philosophy. As C. A. Patrides has pointed out, deification was not expressed even by the Cambridge men in conventional mystical terminology. There is in them no reference to the stages of the mystical life and no analysis of the sufferings or dark nights that the soul endures as it journeys to its goal:

The mysticism of the Cambridge Platonists must be carefully differentiated from the mysticism of other traditions. The shadow of St Theresa or St John of the Cross never fell upon them so as to divert their reason into paroxysms of love. They were never stifled by any 'clouds of unknowing,' they were never tempted to traverse the 'negative way,' and while they borrowed some of the Areopagite's phrases they were never affected by his paradoxical ejaculations or his incandescent language. Their mysticism is perhaps closer to the mysticism of the *Theologia Germanica*. . . . It also has a nominal share in that mysticism which in Pico is joined to a refusal to betray the speculative faculty. But when all is said we must revert once more to Plotinus.[41]

This evaluation by Patrides is exactly true for Traherne. For him also the ultimate union of the soul with God is not an absorption into any form of divine darkness but rather a full waking knowledge by which the soul takes on God's wisdom. In this respect it is a "gnostic" or intellectual mysticism that does, in fact, owe much to Plotinus (205–

70); it also has strong affinities with the speculative mysticism of such men as Meister Eckhart (1260–1328), John Tauler (1290–1361), and Nicholas of Cusa (1401–1464) and is strongly indebted to the Renaissance Platonism of Marsilio Ficino (1433–1499) and Pico della Mirandola (1463–1494), as well as others in the Florentine group. Traherne was, in addition, especially attracted to the writings of the apocryphal Hermes Trismegistus, parts of which were translated by Dr. John Everard (1580–1640) and published in 1650. What interested Traherne (as well as people like Everard) was, of course, the optimism of the Hermetic philosophy. Its identification of the soul with the divine Mind and its consequent emphasis upon the soul's godlike capacity to know all things in a spiritual way were exactly suited to Traherne's own speculative temperament. The speculative mysticism of Traherne is in several ways quite close to the perspective of Hermes, in fact, and Hermes makes an identification between God and man's mind (or soul) that Traherne could accept:

The minde, O Tat, is of the very essence of God, if yet there be any essence of God. What kinde of Essence that is, he alone knows himself exactly. The minde therefor is not cut off or divided from the essentiality of God, but united as the light of the Sun. And this Minde in men, is God.[42]

Long extracts from the 1657 edition of Everard's *Hermes* appear in *Christian Ethicks* and shorter ones are to be found in the *Centuries,* but Traherne may also have known Everard's sermons, first published in 1653 as *Some Gospel Treasures Opened.* These sermons are filled with a highly intellectual mysticism, having its source in such works as Nicholas of Cusa's *The Vision of God* (1453) and in the *Theologia Germanica* (1350?), portions of which, in addition to Hermes, Everard translated. Everard insists upon a strict interpretation of God's absoluteness and thus His identity "in essence" with the Creation and all creatures in it, an identity we can see only with our spiritual eyes: "We see not God in all Places, nor in all Creatures, (as Jacob did then) till our eyes be opened: but God is always in every Creature."[43]

Thus Everard speaks always of the inward meaning of all Christian history, of which the outward events, such as the Crucifixion, are the external symbols. The true spiritual crucifixion goes on eternally within the human soul:

Beloved! I tell you, if you take but this Key, to unlock this Book, this
precious Cabinet of God, you will find precious jewels come tumbling down
to your Hand. Christ Jesus, as he was crucified upon the Cross, so by Way of
Equivalency, he is still and daily crucified in us: For he is *the Lamb, slain from
the Beginning of the World,* Rev. 13.8 and shall be to the End of the World. You
are deceived, if you think, the Passion of Christ is past, when he had suffered
under *Pontius Pilate.* [44]

Everard was suspected by Charles I and Archbishop Laud of being a
Familist fellow-traveller, and he was probably an ideological influence
on Quakerism. As such, he represents a position that is in some places
too close to Enthusiasm for Traherne to have followed him, for Traherne
maintained a greater distance than Everard did from the possible occult
implications of this kind of mysticism. Traherne's education was too
much influenced by the rational approach of new science for him to be
interested in alchemy in either its physical or its spiritual form. Nor did
he take simplistically the older doctrine of the correspondences between
the microcosm and macrocosm which assumes what Henry's twin
brother, Thomas Vaughn (1621–1666), asserted as late as 1652:
"Whatsoever the greater world contains the like shall you find exquis-
itely exprest in this little World of Man."[45] Traherne saw the "book of
nature," not as an exact mirroring of another world but as a general
expression of God's goodness, power, and beauty; these qualities we can
make a part of our souls by recognizing them in and through their
various appearances in the phenomenal world. Traherne's constant
admonition to enjoy the world is his way of asking us to see and absorb
the wisdom of God, but he offers us no specific correspondences, no
occult resemblances, and certainly no elixir that will provide us with
ultimate health and wisdom. His view of God's "traces" in the world is
an expression of the meditative tradition which is directed toward the
natural world, and it has something in common with Thomas Taylor's
(1576–1633) version of it in *Meditations from the Creatures* (1632):

Thus the creation of the world is a Scripture of God, and the voice of God in
all the creatures, and by them all speaketh unto us alwayes, and every where.
The whole world is his booke: so many pages, as there are severall creatures;
no page is empty, but full of lines; every quality of the creature, is a severall
letter of these lines, and no letter without a part of God's wisdome in it. [46]

But Taylor is more concerned with specific parallels between God and the world than Traherne usually is, and he sees here in "every quality of the creature" a particular line of God's wisdom apparently written out in rather exact and easily discernible terms.

Even in his *Meditations on the Six Days of the Creation,* which was largely taken from another source, Traherne does not dwell much upon the particulars of the world but instead encourages a broad meditative awareness of the spiritual principles manifested in its beauty and operations. As he explains in the *Centuries,*

The Services of Things, and their Excellencies are Spiritual: being Objects not of the Ey, but of the Mind: And you more Spiritual by how much more you Esteem them. Pigs eat Acorns, but neither consider the Sun that gav them Life, nor the Influences of the Heavens by which they were Nourished, nor the very Root of the Tree from whence they came. This being the Work of Angels Who in a Wide and Clear Light see even the Sea that gave them Moysture. And feed upon that Acorn Spritualy, while they Know the Ends for which it was Created and feast upon all these, as upon a World of Joys within it: while to Ignorant Swine that eat the Shell, it is an Empty Husk of no Taste nor Delightfull Savor. (*CM* I.26)

The kind of meditation Traherne recommends thus does not draw upon exact lessons to be read from the moral behavior either of the animals or the elements, but sees instead, in the natural cycle of generation, nourishment, and growth, evidence of spiritual meaning. By knowing these processes and personally realizing their significance as manifestations of God's spiritual purposes, one's soul is made like the angels who see everything "in a Wide and Clear Light." The subject of meditation is to be the natural world, but the method by which it is to proceed is also natural in that it requires no special religious exercises or techniques—only a direct perception of the marvelous services that all things provide.

For Traherne, the more practical and empirical perspective of new science had swept away the older systems of correspondences and occult resemblances as well as the carefully structured methods by which meditation was to be conducted. The old truths remain, however, supported in particular by Neoplatonic metaphysics: God is absolutely one, infinite and eternal, and the soul is made as an image and partaker

of Him. The whole Creation manifests God's love and beauty, and the
soul lives in union with the divine life when it imitates God's own love
and knowledge of the world, for the essence of God is such an act of
knowledge and love:

He is One infinit Act of KNOWLEDG and *Wisdom,* which is infinitly
Beautified with many Consequences of Lov & c. Being one Act of Eternal
Knowledge. . . . We are to be Conformed to the Image of His Glory: till we
becom the Resemblance of His Great Exemplar. Which we then are, when
our Power is Converted into Act, and covered with it we being an Act of
KNOWLEDG and Wisdom as He is. (CM II.84)

## Spiritual Vision and Style

In much the same sense that the Baconian method was designed to
place all wits on a level and thereby make truth open to all, so for
Traherne spiritual truth is open to anyone who will raise the lid of his
ignorance and see: "for herby I perceived that we were to liv the Life of
God: when we lived the tru life of Nature according to Knowledg" (*CM*
III.58). The "mystical" vision is, therefore, not something to be won
by hard moral struggle or by penetration into deep mysteries. Nor is it a
matter of inexplicable grace but rather of a spiritual awakening (as out
of sleep) to behold the glory in which one already lives and moves and
has his being. It is because of this mainly gnostic or intellectual nature
of Traherne's mysticism that, as Francis King has observed, Traherne
rarely writes from the point of view of the active meditative process, as
though he were in the act of searching for ultimate understanding.
Traherne does not provide us with a record of the soul groping for
felicity because in his view such groping is a misunderstanding of the
point. Traherne, instead, provides an account or description of the final
vision from the position of its accomplishment:

Traherne's characteristic writing takes its peculiar tone from the sense, the
resolutely maintained sense, of having found and being possessor of 'the
thing itself.' His explorations are not search, but realization.[47]

King further points out that it is this position of achieved vision from which Traherne writes that makes the Augustinian process of meditation less than satisfactory as a means of analyzing him.[48] Although Louis Martz has provided us with sensitive perceptions of Traherne's thought and feeling, for most of Traherne's work particular meditational structures involving a sense of spiritual progress in which "the mind . . . draws toward an inward understanding of the good"[49] are not especially relevant.

For the same reasons, attempts to analyze Traherne's poetry in the light of some special mystical patterning, either of whole poems or of imagery, have been illuminating but not entirely successful.[50] Traherne's thought is mystical but it is not affective or psychological in method. It is intellectual, a matter of seeing from the position of infinity and eternity, and in the same way that all points on the circumference of a circle are equidistant from the center, so eternity and infinity can be reached from wherever one happens to be in time and space. The way is open, and the truth is to be discerned by looking directly at the world. As a result, Traherne's language and his literary structures are, as Stanley Stewart has said, "open," "additive," and "expansive," but they are not (as he also suggests) "digressive" or "erosive" of temporal boundaries.[51] They are, more pertinently, expressive of Traherne's sense of the closeness of all temporal things to their eternal center, and that center is everywhere, as Traherne points out in the famous formula for God attributed to Hermes.[52] Because Traherne's mind is always on this closeness of all things to God, his frequent failure to follow consistently the structural path he indicates for himself is not a digression from his point but rather a "falling into" the true point from his starting position on the periphery. Structure is for Traherne primarily a device for helping the reader to open the lid of his ignorance and to see into the center, which (if he does) will suddenly appear as immediately present both to him and to everything else. It is not by chance that Traherne's favorite image of God and eternity is the sphere, and his perception of God at the center of all reality enters into nearly everything he wrote, where it becomes the primary source of the repetitive, paralleling style that is his fundamental means of expression.

# Chapter Two
# Christian Ethicks

Traherne was at work on *Christian Ethicks* (1675) during the last few months of his life. Proof of this can be found not far from the end of the book where, in a discussion of Liberality, he refers to the generosity of the will of Orlando Bridgeman, who had died on June 25, 1674. Because Traherne died the following October, we know that the *Ethicks* contains Traherne's thinking in its final, or nearly final, form. It is also a clear expression of his ideas because in it they are not subordinated to meditation or instruction in spiritual progress, as they are in the *Centuries,* the *Thanksgivings,* and the poems, for instance. Thus, the *Ethicks* is an excellent work with which to begin a study of Traherne's thought and art, for it provides the least equivocal expression we have of his major philosophical perspectives, and it gives us those perspectives in a style that we know he was using at the end of his life. This style is not always as disciplined or as pleasing as that in the *Centuries,* but it does not radically differ from the earlier style, and it provides many examples of Traherne's most characteristic prose.

## Cornerstones of Ethical Thought

*Christian Ethicks* presents Traherne's ideas more directly than anything else he wrote, but it is not a systematic statement of his philosophy. Traherne was, after all, a minister in the Church of England whose thinking was founded upon principles of Christian belief, and he made little attempt to clarify those principles or their implications in explicit philosophical terms. Rather, he expressed himself primarily in the language of religion and the metaphysics of Christian Neoplatonism in which areas his thinking moved with ease. The more closely one reads Traherne, in fact, the more one is impressed by the clarity of his metaphysical and mystical understanding. He seems able to see through to the final implications of the ideas he is expressing without becoming lost either in self-doubt or in any of the vexing issues that were engaging the wits of other men. Traherne held a strict monist view, from which perspective the problems of spirit and matter or extension and thought were not genuine, for if the ultimate reality of everything is the single, undivided One, there can be no final distinction between spirit and matter; thus, no question can arise as to where spirit (or soul) is to be found or whether it is possible for purely nonmaterial spirit to influence solid, nonspiritual matter. Traherne saw no essential difference between spirit and matter and recognized through his own insight, supported and enhanced by his reading in Neoplatonism, that the material world is actually the infinite, eternal One viewed in and through the dimensions of time and space. As a Christian Platonist, then, Traherne identified the One of Neoplatonic thought with God, but he did not concern himself with the real or presumed philosophic problems of this identification. Instead, he engaged directly in the pursuit of the mystical union with God that this metaphysic implies.

Although Traherne made no effort to write a systematic explanation of his philosophy, his basic assumptions were, nevertheless, profoundly influential in shaping the structure of *Christian Ethicks*. It is, in fact, Traherne's deep commitment to the oneness of all things in God, Who is infinite and eternal, that led him to elaborate the virtues as so many variations on a single theme: the soul's union with God, or Felicity. As Traherne says in the *Centuries:*

God is the Object, and God is the Way of Enjoying. . . . Eternity and Time, Heaven and Earth, Kingdoms and Ages, Angels and Men, are in him to be enjoyed. In him, the fountain, in him the End; in him the Light, the Life, the Way, in him the Glory and Crown of all. (*CM* V.1)

All the virtues are (in God) thus necessarily only one virtue, as Nicholas of Cusa also asserts from a similar perspective:

Thou mayest in consequence remark how all attributes assigned to God cannot differ in reality, by reason of the perfect simplicity of God, although we in divers ways use of God divers words. But God, being the Absolute Ground of all formal natures, embraceth in Himself all natures. . . . And so all Theology is said to be stablished in a circle, because any one of His attributes is affirmed of another, and to have is with God to be, and to move is to stand, and to run is to rest, and so with the other attributes.[1]

For Traherne, too, all God's attributes are one with each other, and when man has attained union with God, all the separate virtues by which he has attained this union are found to be simply various forms of one single virtue: "VERTUE is a comprehensive Word, by explaining which we shall make the way more easy to the right Understanding of all those particular Vertues, into which it is divided" (*CE,* 23). If all the particular virtues are in this fundamental way but varying expressions of the one virtue that is identical with God, then it is no wonder that all theology should be "stablished in a circle" or that the elaboration of Christian virtues should take place through a kind of dialectical spiral-ling and doubling back upon themselves of phrase upon phrase, word upon word. As one proceeds in his reading of *Christian Ethicks* and tries to grasp its basic organizing principles, he is impressed by this swirl-ing, eddying, reduplicating effect of Traherne's language and the relevance of Stanley Stewart's view of the *Ethicks* as an example of an "Open form" in which changes, additions, and repetitions may take place at any time.[2] This repetitive, incantatory manner also has some similarity to the style of the Quakers, who were most active from 1650 to 1675, the period of Traherne's mature life,[3] and the style is more than likely related in part to Traherne's and the Quakers' mutual concern for an inward truth, an intense desire to speak of the direct experiencing of God, and a concentration upon "naming" as the expression of reality.[4]

But Traherne's style and organizational methods in the *Ethicks* do not arise essentially or simply in order to reflect a sense of wonder or to suggest a feeling of communion or unity between souls, or even to describe an "indescribable" mystical experience.[5] These purposes exist, but they are secondary to the influence of Traherne's Neoplatonic vision of the oneness of all things in the Mind of God (the Intelligible World) wherein past and future, every object and every virtue exist in a simultaneous present. Such an idea of an eternal present is a com-monplace of Neoplatonism and mysticism, though variously expressed.

Thomas Stanley (1625–1678), who provided the seventeenth century with a popular description of various philosophic doctrines, explains the Intellect as that which contemplates the intelligible ideas and quotes Pico's statement that in platonic philosophy the Ideas in the Divine Mind constitute the Intelligible World:

Hereupon they say, though God produced only one creature, yet he produced all, because in it he produced the Ideas and forms of all, and that in their most perfect being, that is the Ideal, for which reason they call this Mind, the Intelligible World.[6]

And John Norris (1657–1711), a later Cambridge Platonist and follower of Nicholas Malebranche (1638–1715), makes the concept of the Intelligible World a fundamental part of his philosophy and provides an important description of it as the timeless presence of all things in their ideal state:

By the *Ideal* State of things, I mean that state of them which is necessary, permanent and immutable, not only Antecedent and Prae-existent to this, but also Exemplary and Representative of it, as containing in it Eminently and after an intelligible Manner, all that is in this Natural World, according to which it was made, and in Conformity to which all the Truth, Reality, Order, Beauty and Perfection of its Nature does Consist, and is to be Measured. The System of things existing after this manner, is what we call the *Ideal World,* which is not a Contingent, Temporary, Mutable thing, as this, but a self Existing, Eternal, Necessary and Immutable Nature, really Simple and One, but yet vertually and eminently Multiform and Various.[7]

As Norris tells us, far from implying that the oneness of things fuses all reality into an indistinguishable sameness, this concept understands reality as one in God but at the same time both simple (or undifferentiated) and infinitely rich with variety and beauty. God in His essence is one simple Being but in His manifestation is, mysteriously, the ground and source of the glorious multifariousness of the universe. Although Traherne does not always speak directly of the Intelligible World by name, the idea of it is basic to his thought. God is a simple Being, Whose essence and act are one, and it is because of this simplicity that He is able to be all things:

We must take heed of conceiving GOD to be one Thing, and his Act another, for all his Wisdom and Goodness, all his Blessedness, and Life, and Glory are in the Act, by which he became the Fountain and the End of all Things. (*CE*, 67)

Thus, as we have noted earlier, in the same way that all points on the circumference of a circle are equally distant from the center, so all things in the Creation are equally distant from God, their center, and if it is examined with the proper understanding, anything whatever, any concept or virtue, can lead one back to God, the ultimate reality. That is why Traherne must establish his theology in a circle, why he cannot help naming and renaming, piling synonyms and parallel phrases upon each other in a continuous round of what, from one perspective, are apparent digressions and repetitions. Yet Traherne wants to present to his reader more than the magnificence and beauty of the Creation and more even than the awesomeness of a Creator who ought to be loved and obeyed because He is powerful. He wants, rather, to make us grasp directly the still more awesome but joyous truth that when we touch and see and feel the world around us and within us we are actually experiencing God Himself manifested in the world. This truth is, in fact, verified by the doctrine of the Intelligible World which affirms that the entire universe of time and space is paradoxically both God (if we consider its ultimate Being) and not God (if we consider it only in its individual nature). As John Norris explains, all things exist simultaneously and together as ideas in the Mind of God at the same moment that we see them here, existing also in a limited but nonetheless real fashion. Because of this simultaneity of all things both as infinite and finite, Traherne is willing to begin at any point and shift to any other point that may seem relevant for displaying the world before us and making us become aware of the wondrous fact that all things are expressions of God's eternal Mind.

Because of the force of this desire to demonstrate the true spiritual nature of everything to his reader, Traherne is generally impatient with preconceived forms and is best when his main design can arise more or less organically from a spontaneous flow of thought and word. This is particularly well illustrated by *Christian Ethicks* where, although he begins with the intention of following a systematic analysis of the virtues, he almost immediately abandons most of his system for a largely free, associational pattern of discussion that mixes categories, adds items as they occur to him, and silently drops others that have been previously proposed.

## The Structural Design

Traherne's design for the *Ethicks* is patterned after the same broadly Aristotelian-Scholastic approach to the virtues taken by most Renaissance works on ethics.[8] But this Aristotelian framework soon grows dim under the layers of Traherne's Neoplatonic and speculaive rhetoric: the piling up of synonyms, the repetitions, and the parallel syntactic structures that seek to disclose the center of his thought.

First, Traherne spends two chapters explaining his general purpose, which is, as he says:

To elevate the *Soul,* and refine its Apprehensions . . . to enrich the Mind, and guide Men . . . in the way of *Virtue;* . . . to encourage them to Travel, to comfort them in the Journey, and so at last to lead them to true Felicity, both here and hereafter. (*CE, 3*)

And he defines virtue in general as *"a Right and well order'd Habit of mind, which Facilitates the Soul in all its operations, in order to its Blessedness"* (*CE,* 25). But prior to this definition he outlines the virtues according to the usually accepted scheme in moral treatises, dividing "virtuous Habits" into Theological, Intellectual, Moral, and Divine (*CE,* 23). In enumerating the theological virtues (his first subdivision), however, he begins to add to virtues as the need seems to arise. Apparently trusting his own mind and experience to guide him to the truth rather than the authority of the theologians (in the spirit of Glanvill's boast that "Authorities alone with me make no *number,* unless Evidence of Reason stand before them"),[9] Traherne is not content with the division of the theological virtues into only Faith, Hope, and Charity but immediately adds a fourth, Repentance, which he explains "is chiefly taught by the Word of GOD, and respects GOD as its Principal Object" (*CE,* 23).[10] Then, apparently pulled somewhat off his intended path by his intuition that in an ultimate sense *all* virtues have God as their principal object, Traherne decides to mention three more that could be listed as theological. "If we are making them more," he says, "we may add *Obedience,* Devotion, Godliness" (*CE,* 23), but he says no more about these added virtues later in the work.

The next group, the intellectual virtues, receives even less specific attention, for after listing the usual five—Wisdom, Intelligence, Science, Prudence, and Art—he remarks that because distinctions between them are too subtle for the average reader he will "reduce them perhaps to a fewer number" (*CE,* 23). As it turns out, he does not reduce them but neglects any further discussion of the intellectual virtues altogether. It is possible that this neglect could be in part the result of his placing both Wisdom and Prudence in two different categories of virtues at the same time. Wisdom is an intellectual as well as a divine virtue, while Prudence is an intellectual as well as a principal moral virtue. But Traherne is not the only one to engage in such ambiguous classification. The same double appearance of Prudence is found in the scheme of no less an intellectual architect than Thomas Aquinas,[11] and as Aristotle admits in his *Nicomachaen Ethics,* "precision is not to be sought for alike in all discussions."[12] Traherne at least does not make the problem any more difficult than it already is, for it is only as a moral virtue that he actually discusses Prudence later in the book, having treated it as an intellectual virtue merely by calling it "that knowledge, by which we guide ourselves in Thorny and *uncertain* affairs" (*CE,* 24). Traherne is, nonetheless, neither an Aquinas nor an Aristotle, and rigorous divisions are far less important to him than reminding the reader of the one divine source that lies at the center of all the virtues.

This movement toward the center continues as he takes up the divine virtues: *"Wisdom, Knowledge, and Truth,"* which "have not only GOD for their Object and End, [as do the theological virtues] but their Pattern and Example" [which the theological virtues do not have] (*CE,* 24). By practicing the divine virtues, he says, "we also are changed into the same Image, and are made partakers of the Divine Nature" (*CE,* 24). He further describes his plan by adding virtues to the category now at hand. To the initial three divine virtues he adds Goodness, Righteousness, and Holiness, "All which," he asserts cryptically, "will appear in *Divine Love,* in more peculiar manner to be handled" (*CE,* 24). He apparently does not mean to classify Divine Love as one of the virtues, but Traherne's tendency to trust his own intuitive reason and to move beyond the structures of things to the ideas that underlie them is again revealed in this new addition to the lists. And it is revealed further when later in the book he begins to develop his explanations of the virtues themselves. In predictable fashion he discusses the divine virtues first, but he is scarcely launched when he finds that he must include some account of how Knowledge is obtained and how it must first be moved by a desire or love of Knowledge before the soul will seek it. He follows his chapter on Knowledge by one on Love and its relation to Hatred and moves immediately after this to Divine Love itself, whereupon he takes up the remaining divine virtues as he has earlier listed them: Truth, Wisdom, Righteousness, Goodness, and Holiness, in that order. But without warning he changes direction, apparently through association with the immediately preceding discussion of Holiness, which ends:

GOD, therefore may be infinitely Holy, and infinitely desire our Righteous Actions, tho he doth not intermeddle with our Liberty, but leaves us to our selves; having no Reserve but his Justice to punish our ofences. (*CE*, 93)

With this reference to Justice in his mind Traherne decides to include Justice as one of the divine virtues, and he begins the next chapter with an explanation of his sudden change of plan:

THO following the common Course of Moralists, in our Distribution of Vertues, we have seated *Justice* among the Cardinal *Moral;* yet upon second Thoughts we find reason to reduce it to the number of *Divine* Vertues, because upon a more neer and particular Inspection, we find it to be one of the Perfections of GOD, and under that notion shall discover its Excellence far more compleatly, then if we did contemplate its Nature, as it is limited and bounded among the Actions of Men. (*CE*, 94).

Again, because in God Justice is tempered with Mercy, Traherne, once more disregarding his earlier plan, discusses Mercy as a divine virtue in the chapter that follows Justice. Thus, from an original three, Traherne's divine virtues have grown by one means or another to eight (not counting Divine Love), and this rather remarkable freedom with which he treats them is typical of his method throughout the *Ethicks*. For example, from his list of the "Principal (or Cardinal) Moral" virtues of Prudence, Justice, Temperance, and Fortitude he later removes Justice and adds Courage (a synonym for Fortitude, perhaps), Patience, Meekness, Humility, and Contentment. Finally, he discusses only four of the nine "Less Principal" virtues he had first listed (he treats Magnanimity, Modesty, Liberality, and Magnificence) and spends the last two chapters on Gratitude, which he had not previously mentioned as a virtue at all.

Such, then, is the general structure of *Christian Ethicks:* it begins with an overall design based on the system of virtues inherited from Aristotle's *Nichomachean Ethics* and filtered through Thomas Aquinas and centuries of Christian thought, but under the pressure of his preoccupation with the simultaneity of all things as manifestations of the Divine Mind Traherne soon ignores his organizational plan and begins to move in something like epicycles around the true center of his concern, which is the ultimate union of the soul with God in knowledge and love. All virtues both lead to and are, finally, the same as that union; thus, Traherne adds and subtracts, moving freely from one virtue to the next and shifting the categories of virtues almost as the associations in his mind determine. As he begins more and more to express his own intuitive understanding of the relation each virtue has to the understanding of the Mind of God and how each virtue contributes to the soul's becoming a "Partaker of the Divine nature [and] filled with all the Fulness of God" (*CE*, 22), he creates a series of nearly separate developmental units eddying around a deeply felt central idea. It is because this unifying idea is so strong that the book is, for all its shifts in direction and sudden alterations, not genuinely disordered or chaotic but has, rather, much the same structural character as a theme and variations in music. A theme is stated: virtue is a habit that puts the soul in godlike frame and brings it to the felicity of divine similitude. This theme is then elaborated upon in a series of various statements that stretch it out, shorten it, change its tonality, and ornament it with repeated notes. The circling, repetitive, and freely shifting discussions of the individual virtues are but variations on the central theme: to become godlike by the attainment of that highest virtue, to know and love all things in their infinite, eternal existence in the Intelligible World or Mind of God.

## The Philosophy of the *Ethicks*

What is finally most important for Traherne in *Christian Ethicks* is not the particular arrangement of the virtues, their specific definitions, or their exact relation to each other. Traherne does not concentrate upon any of these things but circles constantly, in the manner of Cusa, around the nature of God, the soul, and how the soul achieves its ultimate felicity. In his thought it is fundamental that God is the one abstract, spiritual essence rather than a personal father. God, who is immutable, infinite, and eternal, is not "part of" time and space, though immanent and onmipresent in time and space. Of this simplicity of God Traherne speaks numerous times throughout the *Ethicks* (and his other works), sometimes using the language of Scholasticism ("IN GOD, to *Act* and to *Be,* are the same Thing" [*CE,* 76]), sometimes the language of Christian love (*"GOD is Love:* . . . his Essence is an infinite and Eternal Act of Love" [*CE,* 50]), and sometimes the language of metaphysics ("we infinitely wrong him, while we limit his Essence to one single Infinity; Who is every way Infinite, in Himself, in all his Works, in all his Waies, . . . in every one of his Perfections" [*CE,* 179]). As Traherne fully understands, it is this very infinite and eternal nature of God that makes possible His omnipresence:

So that in one Instant he can fill both Eternity and Time with enjoyments, Every Part and Particle of which shall be infinitely Delightful, because of the vigor of his Eternal Power in every Operation. Thus is he intirely Acting in Heaven, and Earth, and Hell, at the same time, and at all conceivable Distances beyond all Heavens ever Acting, because he is Willing, Decreeing, seeing and ruling there, and every where accomplishing his Counsel and Pleasure. His Essence and his Will are both the same, his Essence is his Act, and his Act his Pleasure. . . . We must take heed of conceiving GOD to be one Thing, and his Act another. (*CE,* 67)

And it is this same "spiritual" nature that (finally) makes clear the Neoplatonic concept of the Intelligible World, for if God is a simple essence, eternal and infinite, the source of all and omnipresent to all, then all things must exist simultaneously in Him, as His essence; and in that essence, therefore, all past and future are one and the same and all opposites are resolved. This is the Intelligible World. Traherne speaks fully of this idea in the Fifth Century of *Centuries of Meditations* as well as in the "Select Meditations," but his statements in the *Ethicks* are most frequent and clear:

But if it be confessed that Eternity is an everlasting Moment, infinite in duration, but permanent in all its parts, all Things past, present, and to come, are at once before him, and eternally together. (*CE*, 184)

It is a conception of God and eternity that is fundamental in the tradition of Neoplatonism, being shared by other Neoplatonists— Peter Sterry (1613–1672), for example, who also looked to "Plotinus, Origen and Nicholas of Cusa."[13] It is in fact the same essential concept of eternity as that of Beothius (c. 480–523), who, in one of its most impressive expressions, popularized it for the Middle Ages. So too the great German mystic, Meister Eckhart, speaks:

For the Now-moment, in which God made the first man and the Now-moment in which the last man will disappear, and the Now-moment in which I am speaking are all one in God, in whom there is only one Now.[14]

Nicholas of Cusa's thought is filled with the same doctrine; what he says in *The Vision of God* is characteristic:

Thus, Lord, I perceive that naught existeth posterior to thy concept, but that all things exist because Thou dost conceive them. Thou conceivest in eternity, but in eternity succession is without succession, 'tis eternity's self, 'tis Thy very Word, O Lord God. Thou hast no sooner conceived aught that appeareth to us in time than it is. For in eternity in which Thou conceivest, all succession in time coincideth in the same NOW of eternity. There is no past nor future where future and past are one with the present.[15]

In this conception of "all Things past, present, and to come [existing] at once before him, and eternally together," is also the assumption that because the soul is an "image of God" it is able to attain the same vision of "all Things" in the "NOW of eternity" that God has and is. As Traherne says immediately after his own words about eternity existing all at once before God, "[This] is the true Reason, why Eternity is a standing Object before the Eye of the Soul, and all its parts, being full of Beauty and Perfection, for ever to be enjoyed" (*CE*, 184). Such an assumption strongly suggests, of course, that the soul is something more than metaphorically the image of God, that there is an identity "in essence" between God and the soul, though that identity is often expressed equivocally in the Christian and Neoplatonic mysticism that influenced Traherne. Cusa, again, who through Giordano Bruno's influence had much to do with the form in which Neoplatonic mysticism entered the culture of England,[16] seems to accept the essential identification of the Aristotelian "active intellect" with God—a matter about which there had been much debate throughout the medieval period. Cusa identifies the Intellectual Nature as such with God: "Thou [God] art very Sweetness, the Being of life, and intellect," and later demonstrates that this Intellect is the same as man's soul when he says, "Now the intellectual nature, when it quickeneth or animateth the body, is called the human soul."[17] Leone Ebreo (c. 1460–1530), who wrote one of the most popular and influential love treatises of the Renaissance, also makes the identification between the Intellect and God:

The Active Intellect, which gives light to our power of understanding, is God Most High; and hence . . . happiness lies in cognition of the Divine Intellect . . . He is the Supreme Intellect, from which all intellect, activity, form and perfection derive. To Him all things tend, as to their most perfect end; in Him they subsist without multiplication or division, in utter simplicity and unity.[18]

Among others in Traherne's century, Peter Sterry was impressed with Ebreo, and it is probable that Traherne also knew Ebreo's work. But, beyond Ebreo's possible influence upon Traherne's thinking, there is, as we have already seen, the positive influence of Hermes Trismegistus, who, in the Everard translation which Traherne used, speaks explicitly of the mind's being one in essence with God in Whose infinite richness the soul is able to participate.[19] In the *Ethicks,* Traherne, in fact, had begun speaking of and quoting from Hermes shortly before he wrote:

For a distinction may be made between the *Soul,* and *Mind.* The Soul of Man is the immutable essence, or form of his Nature, unimployed. His power of Reasoning is alive, even then when it is quiet and unactive; and this is his Soul. It is one and the same in all men, and of it self equally inclined to all

great and transcendent things: but in the most it is misguided, baffled and
suppressed, and though it be never so great it is to no purpose. . . . His
mind is Good that intendeth well, his mind is Evil that designeth mischief.
So that the Mind is the Soul exerting its power in such an act. (CE, 231–32)

The distinction between the soul and the mind that Traherne makes
here not only owes much to Hermes but also resembles that described in
Zen Buddhism between the hand and the fist. The fist is in one sense (in
and of itself) nothing, but it is at the same time really the hand, the
hand in a particular form or mode of activity. Similarly, to Traherne,
soul and mind are the same in essence, but when the soul is exerted in a
specific "act" of understanding, the condition or "illusion" of a separate
entity (the mind) arises. The soul is, as unexerted, "one and the same in
all men" and identified by Traherne here and elsewhere as the "power of
Reasoning."

   Thus the soul is ("in essence") pure intellectual power existing in an
inactive state. Traherne says at several places in the Ethicks that "REA-
SON, . . . is the Formal Essence of the Soul of Man" (CE, 14, 141), and
such an identification means that any particular act of "reason" or
understanding is the mind itself, that is, simply a specific condition of
the soul. We thus can speak of a man being of this or that mind when he
believes or thinks a certain way, and this condition of mind is, as
Traherne explains it, the same thing as a habit or virtue.

   If Traherne does not say unequivocally that the soul and God are
actually identical, he makes many statements that are very close to such
an identification, and his whole metaphysical view demands it:

By nature he hath implanted the Similitude of his power: which we are to
improve by Grace, turning it into Act after his Similitude.
. . . . . . . . . . . . . . . . . . . . . . . . . . . . . . . . . . . . . . . .
His [God's] very Essence is seated in infinite Knowledge. . . . THE understanding Power, which seated in the Soul, is the Matter of that Act wherein
the Essence of Knowledge consisteth.
. . . . . . . . . . . . . . . . . . . . . . . . . . . . . . . . . . . . . . . .
For GOD is the Light of the understanding. (CE, 52, 36, 41)

Although such an identification must have been intended in the Ethicks
and elsewhere in Traherne's work, it is not necessary to establish that in

his philosophy the soul and God are unequivocally one in essence in order to understand the dynamics of how the soul as pure intellectual power—the power of Reasoning, God's image—is to become united to God as His similitude. It is by having the right thoughts or "intellections" of all things that the soul is to become "of the same Mind, with him who is an infinit Eternal Mind" (*CM* II.84). But the thoughts that set the "Mind in frame" are not simply the products of man's temporal condition or the logic of physical relationship. They are the activity of the Intellect or spiritual faculty itself involved in the contemplation of the Intelligible World. And because the mind and this Intellect are related to each other as wave to the sea, the mind need only change its view of things in order to be revealed as the Intellect or soul itself. When this revelation is accomplished, the soul has come to view all things as God views them, from the position of eternity. As mind, the soul has exerted its power to all things properly, giving them their due esteem as infinite and eternal and thereby expanding the soul's condition to that of God's own Mind:

Not as if it were unlawful to desire to be *Like GOD:* but to aspire to the Perfection in a forbidden way, was unlawful . . . . but to know our selves, and in *the strait and divine Way* to come immediately to God, to contemplate him in his Eternity and Glory, is a right and safe Way: for the Soul will by that means be the Sphere of his Omnipresence, and the Temple of the God-head: It will become ETERNITY, as *Trismegistus* speaketh, or ONE SPIRIT with God, as the Apostle. And then it must needs be present with all things, *in Heaven, and in the Earth, and in the Sea,* as GOD is: for all things will be in it, as it were *by Thoughts and Intellections.* (*CE,* 228)

This proper contemplation of God "in his Eternity and Glory" is a matter both of the knowledge or understanding of all things in the Intelligible World and of a love or appreciation of them all according to their proper relation to God's eternal and infinite purposes:

He knoweth nothing as he ought to Know, who thinks he Knoweth any thing, without seeing its Place, and the Manner how it relateth to GOD, Angels and Men, and to all the Creatures in Earth, Heaven, and Hell, Time, and Eternity. (*CE,* 69)

And he explains clearly how this exertion of our power is an act of the understanding toward all things which in turn is also the same as loving or prizing all with due esteem:

But if we excite and awaken our Power, we take in the Glory of all objects, we live unto them, we are sensible of them, we delight in them, we transform our souls into Acts of Love and Knowledge, we proceed out of our selves into all Immensities and Eternities, we render all Things their Due, we reap the Benefit of all, we are Just, and Wise, and Holy, we are Grateful to GOD, and Amiable in being so: We are not divided from, but united to him, in all his Appearances, Thoughts, Counsels, Operations; we adorn our souls with the Beauty of all objects whatsoever, are transformed into the Image of GOD, live in communion with him, nay live in him, and he in us, are made Kings and Priests unto GOD, and his sons forever; . . . We are in a Divine and spiritual Manner made as it were Omnipresent with all Objects (for the Soul is present only by an Act of the understanding) and the Temple of all Eternity does it then becom, when the Kingdom of GOD is seated within it, as the world is in the Eye; while it lives, and feels, and sees, and enjoyes, in every object to which it is extended, its own & its objects Perfection. (*CE,* 52–53)

This long passage summarizes almost the whole of Traherne's concept of the soul and its manner of coming to union with God. It is the basis of his entire analysis of the virtues in *Christian Ethicks* and of his teaching in all of his other works. In the light of it we can see what he means by his constant admonition to enjoy the world, for enjoyment of the world is a matter of seeing into its meaning in eternity, grasping its spiritual "idea" in the Intelligible World, and thus valuing and loving it from the same eternal and infinite point of view as God does. This enjoyment sets the Mind in frame in that it shapes the soul into that form of Mind, or structure of "thoughts and Intellections," that God is:

. . . our Minds are in Frame when our Thoughts are like his. And our Thoughts are then like his when we hav such Conceptions of all objects as God hath, and Prize all Things according to their value. (*CM* I.13)

And because it is the limited, narrowed vision of time and space that prevents our seeing rightly, it is always the expansion of our straitened, temporal mind that Traherne seeks. The soul has the *power* to see all things as God does, but if it is exerted into narrow, limited activity it cannot realize its power. Thus, as Traherne says, "WHEN our own Actions are Regular, there is nothing in the World but may be made conducive to our Happiness," and "Every Vertue . . . must . . . directly or Obliquely tend to our supreme Happiness; upon this dependeth all their Excellency" (*CE, 30*).

Traherne speaks at one point of the various powers that lie behind the virtues. By understanding his distinction between the soul and the mind, we become aware that these powers are simply the various ways the soul (or "Power of Reasoning") is able to exert itself. When it does exert itself in one of these ways, it becomes that particular mind or habit, thus taking on the virtue in question. Traherne, as we have seen, has defined virtue in general as *"A Right and well order'd Habit of mind, which Facilitates the Soul in all its operations, in order to its Blessedness,"* and he has asserted that "THE Powers of the Soul, are not vertues themselves, but when they are clothed with vertuous Operations, they are transformed into Vertues." Therefore, a virtue or habit is a state or condition of mind—a shape into which the soul is "framed"—and meaningful only as it helps reshape the human mind into the infinite, eternal condition of God's Mind. All individual virtues in this light are variations upon virtue in general, that which "directly or Obliquely tend[s] to our supreme Happiness." It is no surprise, then, to find Traherne, at the end of the work, summarizing under the heading of Gratitude all that he has said about the virtues, and with the introduction of Gratitude we come full circle in Traherne's philosophy as it appears in the *Ethicks,* for Gratitude is his general term for a faithful rendering to God of the proper esteem of all things in the light of eternity:

THAT all the business of Religion on GODS part is Bounty, Gratitude on ours, and that this Gratitude is the sphere of all Vertue and Felicity, easily is discerned after the first intimation. Gratitude is all that is to be expressed here upon Earth, and above in Heaven. All our Complacencies in his infinite Highness, all our Delights in his eternal Praises, all our Adorations, Extasies, and Offerings, all our Joyes and Thanksgivings, are but the Feathers and the Wings of that Seraphim in Glory. (*CE, 284*)

This Gratitude is a form of love, and "By Love the Soul is transformed into the Similitude of God" (*CE, 56*); "Godliness is a kind of

GOD-LIKENESS, a divine habit, or frame of Soul, that may fitly be accounted *The fulness of the stature of the Inward Man*" (*CE,* 285). When we have reached this fullness we have reached that union with God that is, in Traherne's mystical, Christian Neoplatonism, the *final* purpose of man's creation. That we should all reach this goal was Traherne's tireless concern, and it is the primary reason that the *Ethicks* takes on the character of a series of variations on a single theme. The rhetorical schems—the parallel structures, the repetitions, the synonymous phrases, the carefully controlled emphases upon key words, and the shifting of that emphasis to different parts of speech—all turn inward upon that doctrinal center.

## Gratitude: The Final Virtue

*Christian Ethicks* is a series of variations on a theme, but even though we have first called its theme the soul's union with God, we can in Traherne's shifting style also call it Gratitude without implying any change in the nature of that theme. As Traherne proceeds toward the end of his book, Gratitude becomes increasingly significant to him as the single word that can express his whole point, subsuming all he has said about the soul's becoming clothed with perfect knowledge and love.

The clothing of the soul with the habit of Gratitude is identical with the soul's union with God, and Gratitude expresses also the special emphasis Traherne gives to becoming fully alive to the gloriousness of the whole Creation. Gratitude is thus a virtue (it does not matter that it remains unclassified) that combines both love and knowledge and implies something of the magnificence of virtue's whole design:

Is not then the Love which a man returneth a Magnificent thing! Certainly if it answers all these preparations and obligations as their end, and be lookt upon as that without which all the Creation is vain and frustrate, it is the most great and marvellous thing in all the World. (*CE,* 252)

That Traherne becomes fully aware of this special character of Gratitude only as he nears the end of his work is demonstrated as much by the obviously growing enthusiasm with which he writes of Gratitude as by his having made no place for it in his initial design, scarcely mentioning the word before the next to the last chapter—as though in his own writing he is undergoing a process of discovery. That he sees it as combining and balancing the other essential virtues, Knowledge and Love, is something of which he himself speaks: "Pure Gratitude is so divine a thing, that the Soul may safely wish to be turned *all* into Gratitude. Its Employment and Nature are all one, acknowledgement [Knowledge] and benevolence [Love] united together" (*CE,* 275–76). And he takes special pains to develop the reasoning behind this comprehensive nature of Gratitude by explaining how the value of anything is lost when its worth is not acknowledged and appreciated:

The greatest Benefits we can receive, are but *Abortive,* or rather turned into *Curses,* without a Grateful acknowledgment of them: All Gifts are but *Carkasses* devoid of Life, unless inspired with that *Sence,* which maketh them *Delightful.* . . . They must be conceived in the Mind before they can be transformed into Joy, and be transformed into Joyes before they can produce those Praises which are the musick of the Benefactors Soul, as well as of the Receivers. (*CE, 269–70*)

More clearly than any other word Gratitude helps us grasp some of the special qualities of Traherne's thought that give his Christian Neoplatonism its particular character.

In Traherne, for example, few things have caused more comment than his refreshing, yet seemingly un-Neoplatonic joy in the Creation. This joy may seem to be a contradiction of Neoplatonism and not perhaps quite clearly understood by Traherne himself, but he is hardly alone among Neoplatonic thinkers in recommending a positive love of the world. The Cambridge Platonists were themselves appreciative of the beauty of the world, though none was as rapturous as Traherne, and the two most important Neoplatonists whose thinking lies behind much Christian mysticism, Plotinus and Dionysius the Pseudo-Areopagite (ca. 500), both openly admired the world.[20] Thus Neoplatonism does not necessarily deny value to the physical universe; and in Traherne's mind it explicitly does not. In the *Ethicks* there is no extended discussion of enjoyment in itself, but the idea is pervasive. As we shall see when we discuss the *Centuries of Meditations,* enjoyment is nearly synonymous with esteem, love, and appreciation (Gratitude). As Traherne constantly tells us, we cannot esteem something if we do not recognize its worth, and recognizing its worth is a matter of grasping its use and purpose in eterniy, in the divine Mind. It is not a matter simply of being pleased by things through the senses, for the beasts are able to enjoy things in this way. Man is also to enjoy them spiritualy by his awareness of what they are and what purposes they serve. Thus, real enjoyment does not exclude or reject the physical senses as such, but rather transmutes or "raises" them to a spiritual level and preserves them. To enjoy in this way is to exhibit Gratitude.

The soul, therefore, participates in the senses, not as ends in themselves but as manifestations of that which is their true, spiritual nature. Traherne explains this point in the *Ethicks,* but his clearest statement is in *Centuries of Meditations:*

You never Enjoy the World aright, till you see how a Sand Exhibiteth the Wisdom and Power of God: And Prize in evry Thing the Service which they do you, by Manifesting His Glory and Goodness to your Soul, far more then the Visible Beauty on their Surface, or the Material Services, they can do your Body. Wine by its Moysture quencheth my Thirst, whether I consider it or no: but to see it flowing from his Lov who gave it unto Man. Quencheth the Thirst even of the Holy Angels. To consider it, is to Drink it Spiritualy. (*CM* I.27)

This mode of enjoyment is the same as that activity whereby the soul is made one with God by "thoughts and intellections." Traherne speaks of it in relation to almost every one of the virtues, and it is especially pertinent to Righteousness, for, as he explains, Righteousness values "all things according as their Worth and Merit requires." Here again we see how it is that the virtues can be viewed as variations on Gratitude, for this definition of Righteousness differs only in mode of expression from Gratitude itself, and it is the same with virtue after virtue as he discusses them in the *Ethicks.* As he says:

It [Righteousness] is Fruition and Blessedness, because all the perfection and Goodness of GOD is, with his Kingdome, received into the Soul, by the Righteous esteem of all Objects. It is the Beauty and Glory of the Inward Man, because a voluntary Agent, that does incline himself to such excellent Actions, is highly Amiable and Delightful to be seen; Not only because his soul is tranformed into an *Intelligible World,* transcendent to all that is created, by the *Ideas* of GOD, and his Works erected in the mind, but his *Affections* are framed in a living and incomparable Order, according as every Cause and Object requires. There is something in the Soul of a Righteous man, that fitly answers all Obligations and Rewards, It is tranformed into the Image of GOD in such a sort, that in the *Righteous Act,* which it becomes, GOD for ever dwelleth and appeareth. (*CE,* 75)

The idea of Gratitude thus embodies many important facets of Traherne's thinking. It explains, for example, his frequently discussed concept of a free, uncoerced circulation of light, life, and love from God to man and back to God again, an idea that appears clearly in Traherne's statement that God made man in His image so that man might live in His similitude. It is the enjoyment of all things that perfects the things themselves, and this spiritual enjoyment completes the circulation of love and life that God wishes to communicate. But that circulation must be freely completed by man. Without man's freedom the circulation is broken because the foundation of all genuine enjoyment is an entirely *uncoerced* response for what has been received. As Traherne explains, Gratitude is necessary to the perfecting of the creation, and in a beautiful passage in the *Ethicks* he describes the integral relation between this response to the creation and man's freedom. It is axiomatic that love cannot be forced because force can command only obedience and fear, not the willing devotion which renders joyful service to the beloved.

Although at first glance it might seem that Traherne's emphasis upon the final oneness of all souls with God would nullify man's freedom, such is far from being so. In fact, it is an important tenet in such Neoplatonist/mystical thinking that, as Traherne might have expressed it, the soul (as God's image) is bound by its limited mode of "seeing" in the dimensions of time and space. As image the soul has perfect freedom always in itself, but when the soul is exerted as mind (which in some measure it always is so long as it functions in man), that perfect freedom is reduced to so low a level that it consists of simple choice alone—merely the ability to perceive the good and assent to it—until the soul is able, through strengthening its power of assent, to conform the nature of its exertion (setting the mind in frame) to God's. Only by transcending the perspective of temporality and adopting the vision of infinity–eternity can man bring his act (mind) into conformity with his essence (soul) and thus, by paralleling God's nature, become godlike. There always remains, nonetheless, and, from the standpoint of logic, paradoxically, a tension, if not precisely a distinction, between God and the soul that requires and validates man's being free either to love or to hate without coercion. The idea of freedom is, in fact, vital in Traherne's thinking. Man must be free; if he were not free the Creation would be null and void:

A wise and worthy Benefactor designs the felicity and contentment of the Person, to whom he imparteth his Bounties: and if he were able, would do that for him, which above all other things is most to be desired; not *compel* him to be Grateful, whether he would or no; for that would but spoil the beauty of his Return . . . He has put brave Principles and Inclinations into the Soul of Man, and left him freely to exert them, with infinite desire to see him act freely, but generously and nobly. For by this means only, is he made capable of Honour, and the essence of Gratitude consists in the freedom of its operation. (*CE,* 271)

This free return of Gratitude involves another of Traherne's favorite ideas, that when the individual soul freely completes the intended circulation of Gratitude back to God, a mutual enhancement takes place among all souls. There are several reasons for this. If the Gratitude is a proper expression of love and knowledge, then it involves no condition of personal possession and has nothing to do with marking off anything for itself alone. At the same time, every soul that delights in God and His works in this way is itself like a bright jewel to all other souls, just as acquaintance with a good and honorable person adds value to one's own life. Also, such an outpouring of appreciation will be directed by each soul to all other souls because each is a part of God's gift of the Creation to all. In these ways all souls are linked by love and delight to each other in a glorious communion that is the greater the more souls there are:

THUS, you see, if GOD had given all Eternity and Immensity to a man, if he had made no other Creatures but him alone, his Bounty had been defective: Whereas by the Creation of these he hath filled Eternity and Immensity with Treasures. . . . For every one of them is to Love all his Creatures as he does, and to delight in the Beauty and Felicity of all, . . . And the Greater, and the Richer, and the fairer they are, the more Great and Happy are we. (*CE,* 83)

The paradox of being able to enjoy more things as a result of there being more souls to enjoy them is thus resolved: "THE Existence of many Souls is so far from abating the value of one, that it is by reason of their multitude more useful and Excellent" (*CE,* 38).[21] And the concept that most easily helps us see how that resolution is achieved is expressed with particular succinctness by the one word *Gratitude.* Gratitude, as Traherne himself comes to discover as he writes, "is the sphere of all Vertue and Felicity," and as the *Ethicks* demonstrates throughout, it is Traherne's definition of the whole duty of man.

## The Rhetoric of Gratitude

What Traherne means by Gratitude is a significant indication of his "speculative" or intellectualizing orientation toward the world. As more than one critic has noticed, it is not things but the "thoughts" (proper intellection) of things that interest Traherne;[22] although these thoughts in which he is interested may at first seem remote from the establishment of Gratitude, the two are (finally) the same. They can be seen, also, as an expression of the broader meaning of the whole meditative or contemplative tradition, and in his assertion that the proper thoughts of things have primary importance Traherne is not essentially different from such a man as Sir Thomas Browne (1605–1682), some of whose statements closely resemble Traherne's in point of view if not in style. In the *Religio Medici* (1642), for example, Browne expresses the same concern with man's purpose in studying nature that Traherne does, and he also emphasizes it by reference to the commonplace that beasts are unable to return to God that "devout and learned admiration" of which man is capable:

The world was made to be inhabited by beasts, but studied and contemplated by man: 'tis the debt of our reason we owe unto God, and the homage we pay for not being beasts. Without this, the world is still as though it had not been, or as it was before the sixth day, when as yet there was not a creature that could conceive or say there was a world. The wisdom of God receives small honour from those vulgar heads that rudely stare about, and with a gross rusticity admire his works. Those highly magnify him whose judicious enquiry into his acts, and deliberate research of his creatures, return the duty of a devout and learned admiration.[23]

In whatever one studies, then, his final purpose should be to return to God this devout and learned admiration, not to increase his power over the world or to manipulate it for individual profit. One's real duty is simply to esteem the whole of the Creation as God made it, to appreciate all things in their places as God intended them to be. It is this understanding of man's ultimate duty that marks a significant difference between the new scientist and the traditional religious or meditative thinker, for to seek knowledge of the world in order to engage in a learned admiration would cut short the gathering of knowledge, and to the Cambridge Platonists observation and thinking *were* confined to an ultimately meditative purpose.[24]

This same purpose generates in Traherne its own special form of rhetoric, a rhetoric that is continually shifting in its individual parts but constant in its revelation of the underlying unity of all things beneath the changing surfaces. The reader's attention is directed toward everything simultaneously. Like a juggler keeping torches spinning before our eyes, Traherne presents a dazzling display of verbal lights and colors to the reader: strings of nearly synonymous words shifting from nouns to verbs to adjectives, parallel phrases and clauses emphasizing a key word in repetition, and rapid changes in metaphor that may end in paradox, all leading the reader toward a heightened perception in which he sees into the richness and fullness of the infinite, eternal one. What Stanley Fish has written of Browne's *Religio Medici* thus applies also to Traherne's *Ethicks,* though in a somewhat different way from that which Fish shows is applicable to Browne:

In a word, the prose *resolves,* and what it resolves is, "all things into God" . . . . the *Religio Medici*['s]. . . structure imitates the *uni*verse it celebrates, a conglomeration of "singular essences" (divided pieces) each of which bears a uniform significance.[25]

According to Fish's stimulating analysis, Browne, unlike Herbert or Donne, does not seek to change his reader's mind and make him a better man but rather asks the reader to forget the difficult questions of life and to have confidence that all will be well without any alteration in the nature of the self. Browne is, therefore, a "bad physician" in the uses of his prose, while such writers as Donne, Herbert, Bacon, and Bunyan are "good physicians" because they shock the reader's self-complacency "in the hope that [the resulting] self-knowledge will be preliminary to the emergence of a better self."[26] The physician metaphor is not only traditional but extremely helpful in understanding the rhetoric of Gratitude in the *Ethicks* and Traherne's other work. Traherne participates in the same general tradition as Browne, Donne, Herbert, and Bunyan of "asking the rational understanding to abdicate in favor of the revealed word," and he also "denies" the "distinction between God and everything else,"[27] but it is in neither of the ways Fish assigns to these writers that Traherne seeks to accomplish his intentions. He does not offer the reader "an uncomfortable and unsettling experience"[28] (the tortures of hell or the evils of sin) nor does he soothe the reader's troubled soul. Rather, Traherne attempts to change the reader into a new self by presenting him with so vast and irresistibly attractive a vision that he will inevitably be turned into perfect love and knowledge.

To account fully for this special character of Traherne's rhetorical strategy one needs perhaps to combine the perspectives of both Stanley Stewart and Fish, for their analyses taken together provide an insight into Traherne's technique that has not been entirely available before. Stewart's metaphor of "expansion" is, for example, very much to the point, for although Stewart does not relate Traherne's "expanded voice" fully to the specific Christian-Neoplatonic metaphysic that underlies this expansion, it is obvious that the thrust of Traherne's language is always outward toward the largest vision possible—toward infinity. Regarding this character of Traherne's style Stewart's perceptions are most helpful:

In Traherne's mature prose style "openness" is the defining characteristic of the speaker's point of view. The dominant voice is that of an anti-character, an egoless being whose soul expands by a process of perfect narcissism, one who, like the loose syntax of the work itself, bears no limits of space or time. Hence, the author tries to erode the expected distinction between author and audience, just as he tries to destroy the integrity of beginning, middle, and end.[29]

Stewart thus sees this expansiveness as a process of "erosion" or "destruction" in which the "integrity" of time and space is violated.

But if we are to understand Traherne's motivations properly, we must change the images of destruction and erosion to transcendence and freedom, for Traherne's most fundamental point throughout all his work is that, in a spiritual sense, boundaries and limitations are illusions that are seen through once knowledge has come. To speak of the limits of space and time, the distinctions between author and audience, or the integrity of beginning, middle, and end, as Stewart does, is to speak as though these conditions ought to be preserved and thus to appear to argue for the rightness of error or the integrity of ignorance, as if error and ignorance should be protected against the destructive power of truth and knowledge. The belief in separate, real distinctions on the temporal level is exactly that form of error or ignorance that Traherne insists men must overcome, for it is ignorance that causes our spiritual sickness, constrains our Gratitude, and absents us from our Felicity. If we follow his argument we will see that our notion of limits, or distinctions, beginnings, middles, and ends is, on a spiritual level, only an illusion—a mistake in the true identity of reality, a mistake which is done away with at the coming of knowledge, just as darkness disappears with the coming of dawn.

The proper figure for the process through which Traherne is leading his reader is, therefore, not one of destruction or erosion but of awakening, of opening the "lid of ignorance" so that the spiritual eye may clearly see and flood the soul with light. This is the method by which Traherne intends to effect the reader's cure, and for this reason Fish's metaphor of the physician is a cogent one even though its connotations of pathology and the pain of treatment are for Traherne somewhat misleading. Traherne does not ask the soul to swallow any bitter pills of recognition of its sinful condition because such bitterness and sense of sin arise from the very ignorance that he is trying to convert into knowledge. To recognize that one is sitting in darkness and to feel the pain of such recognition may be a first step toward moving into the light, but it is not the move itself, and if ignorance (the notion that the world and the soul are really separate things, divided and distinguished from God) constitutes that darkness, then knowledge commits no painful surgery but simply transforms the soul. Traherne, in fact, makes it clear that the cure he contemplates does not come about either through any purging of the soul or through destroying the "integrity" of "distinctions" between things (distinctions themselves are ignorance). As he explains, the cure is only a matter of flooding the soul with light. Like a mirror that is filled with the sun, the soul becomes filled with God and is completely changed:

WERE there no SUN it were impossible for so fair an *Idea* to be conceived in a Mirror, as is sometimes in a Glass, when it is exposed to the skie. . . . Yet now [since] there is a Sun, the Matter is easie, 'tis but to apply it to the face of the Sun, and the Glass is transformed. And if GOD dwelleth in the Soul as the Sun in a Mirror, while it looketh upon him, the love of GOD must needs issue from that Soul, for *GOD is love,* and his love is in it. The impression of all his Beauty swallows up the Being of the Soul, and changes it wholly into another nature. (*CE,* 264)

This passage is the real key to Traherne's method of curing the soul as well as to the basis of the soul's expansion and the rhetoric of Gratitude that expresses and achieves that cure. What Traherne will do is expose the soul to God by holding it up to the Creation as to a mirror in which His beauty and love shine forth, and the soul, thus applied "to the face of the Sun," will be transformed into God. It would be difficult to find a better description of what are for Traherne the uses of meditation or contemplation, for the most important function of either is to fix the ultimate spiritual meaning of what is "thought about" fully and firmly in the soul—to fill the soul with meaning and to transform the soul by it. To accomplish this by means of words one need simply call the whole world—its infiniteness, its eternality, and its divine beauty—to the reader's attention. Thus, Traherne continually names the glorious and voluminous riches of the world in and through which we can perceive God's divine essence. At the same time that he holds the reader's soul up to the inexhaustible beauty and richness of things, Traherne wants the reader to perceive that he and all things are directly within, made up of and surrounded by, infinity and eternity. At the center of this whole vision of the world is the paradox that all the richness, all the glorious and beautiful things in the temporal world, are but one thing—God Himself appearing in infinitely various ways. Traherne's language reflects this mysterious paradox of the infinity of "temporal" things by constantly transforming the concreteness of the things he names to their "idea," so that they appear as abstractions or symbols of their spiritual principles. By continually moving from name to name as well as by constantly shifting the logical-temporal relationships between these names—rapid changes in metaphor, avoidance of clear position-ing in time and space—Traherne suggests further the paradoxically simultaneous presence of all things, all times, and all space in the Mind of God.

Immediately before the Appendix of the *Ethicks* Traherne writes a long, impassioned paragraph that illustrates the special qualities of his rhetoric by which he would be the good physician and cure the soul. He is discussing the nature of Gratitude, how it is a form of love or esteem for benefits known, and he moves to a summing up of what this crown of all the virtues will do for the one who has it. As he warms to his subject, Traherne employs an impressive array of rhetorical devices. Small patterns of naming—of repetition—are contained within larger patterns; the temporal logic of the naming is continually moving from concrete space-time to the abstract, simultaneous, and infinite, and the passage culminates in the paradox that each soul's possession of the world actually increases the possession of every other soul. Like love, which is increased by being given away, this spiritual possession is increased the more it is used. This paradox is "the great Mystery of Blessedness and Glory," and although it may seem at first glance to be a form of narcissism, as Stewart terms it, there is nothing narcissistic about it. On the contrary, it involves a forgetting of the egocentric or personal self and an absorption into the totally ego-less "Self" of God that pours out love toward everything without compromise. Traherne's language flows out in imitation of this same abundance as he ad-monishes his reader not to love in some narrow, personal fashion:

HE that praiseth GOD only for his Health, and Food, and Rayment, and for his blessing on his Calling (as too many only do) either is very ignorant, or upon a strict scrutiny, will be detected for upbraiding GOD, for the meanest of his bounty. For his Love must infinitely be defective, that is able to bestow Gifts infinitely more, yet giveth us none but these. He that sees not more Causes of Joy than these, is blind and cannot see afar off: The very truth of

Religion is obscure to him, and the cause of Adoration unknown. He wanteth ten thousand demonstrations of the Love of GOD, and as many Incentives to enflame his Soul in the Return of Love, that is unacquainted with these high and mighty bounties. No man can return more Blessings than he receiveth: nor can his Praises exceed the number (and greatness) of his Joyes. A House is too little, a Kingdom is too narrow for a Soul to move in. The World is a confinement to the power, that is able to see Eternity, and conceive the Immensity of Almighty GOD! (*CE,* 276)

The thought of this section of the paragraph (the whole paragraph fills a page and a half) is based upon self-evident principles: if one is not aware of what he has been given, he can hardly be grateful for it, and to the extent that he is not grateful he will be narrow-minded and miserable, a mean-spirited and selfish, or, at best, sentimental person. He will upbraid God for having given him only what little he sees around him in his narrow vision of things, and he will think, "if God is perfect love and able to do all things, why has he given me so little?"

Traherne's answer to this is, of course, that such a person simply does not see what God has given and, content with merely temporal things, is ignorant of God's gift of Himself in his infinite eternal richness. To understand this, one must lift the eyes of his soul out of the confines of his purely personal self (his physical well-being, health, clothing, food, job, and social position) and direct them toward the spiritual realities of the universe.

The syntax of the first sentence is straightforward and does not subvert itself as Fish says is the way of the self-consuming artifact,[30] but in the opening clause the naming of things in series is given an added emphasis by the repetition of "and" as well as by shifting the pattern of the last item to lengthen that pattern with a near rhyme and a hint of alliteration: "his blessing on his Calling." All this calls the reader's attention to the separateness of each item, the isolation of each from every other, and the subsequent lack of significance each has in relation to the universe. The items named are only "the meanest [examples] of [God's] bounty," and they are therefore given a per-functory treatment, a bare listing without emotional coloring. Their separateness from any larger meaning is further enhanced by the neutral conjunction "and" which presents them without stating any relation-

ship of one to another. The negative effect upon one's thinking that a
narrow perspective will have is next expressed by making the reader
picture a potentially generous and bountiful love being constrained by
an arbitrary withholding of what might have been provided. Surely a
God who was able to do infinitely more but who has done nothing but
to provide us with "Health and Food, and Rayment" and a job to work
at can hardly be worthy of profound Gratitude. "He that praiseth God"
for such shallow reasons simply does not know enough about what God
has actually done and is by his ignorance actively insulting God—
putting restraints upon Him by not letting Him give to the soul those
infinite spiritual gifts that He is in fact always offering to it. It is the
ignorance of these gifts that prevents their realization, and Traherne
does not want the reader to dwell upon bad examples but to turn away
from all concern with the self as soon as possible.

When, in fact, he repeats the structure of the opening clause to
continue the examples of faulty praise ("He that sees not more causes of
Joy than these"), the force of the negative is intentionally weak, and it is
soon nearly forgotten as Traherne presses home what it *is* that the
shortsighted person cannot see. Thus, Traherne shifts the focus of
attention away from examples of ignorant, narrow thinking onto those
great and abundant gifts that are waiting to be recognized, and one is
carried along by the flow of riches streaming from God's love.

Because Traherne explains this bounty as "the very truth of Religion"
and "the cause of Adoration" the reader is hardly concerned that these
things are "obscure" or "unknown" to the ignorant man. What he
begins to feel and remember is that there are "ten thousand demonstrations of the Love of GOD" and that his soul should be and can be
enflamed by love. Before he is fully aware of the logic of the statements,
the reader's vision is becoming expanded to take in (absorb) the infinity
of blessings God has provided. Traherne's syntax is direct and simple,
bearing plainly his deeper meaning as he reiterates the obvious principle upon which his argument is based: No man can be grateful for what
he is ignorant of. That there are in fact ten thousand demonstrations of
God's love Traherne does not try to prove by logic but by providing
these demonstrations directly; and as he prepares to do so he echoes the
vastness of the soul's capacity, moving outward by a series of increas-

ingly larger perspectives, from House, to Kingdom, to World, to Eternity, and finally to the Immensity of God.

From the narrow perspective of one who looks to God simply as a personal benefactor providing the comforts of daily life Traherne has expanded the reader's view outward to infinity—an infinity that is not empty but full, rich, and overflowing with splendor. The movement has been accomplished by Traherne's reiterative manner in which the structural patterns of phrases and clauses are repeated with sometimes subtle variations and skillfully placed stresses upon key words so that we experience them now as simultaneous items in the Intelligible World and now as ascending steps toward eternity and infinity.

But what we have seen so far is only a third of the paragraph. Once Traherne has begun to move the reader toward a vision of eternity and infinity, he begins another movement in which he demonstrates what the effects of such a vision will be upon the one who has it. The rhetorical link between these movements in the paragraph is the continued repetition of the phrase "He that . . ." which turns from negative to positive examples and becomes the larger frame for various smaller units of repetition, parallelism, and ascending stress. As the larger frame continues to encompass and support the smaller units, Traherne focuses attention upon adverb, noun, adjective, and back to noun again in a richly varied pattern of rhetorical emphases. The paragraph continues:

He that can look into infinite Spaces, must see them all full of delights, or be infinitely displeased. How like an Angel doth he soar aloft, how divine is his life, how glorious and heavenly; that doth converse with infinite and eternal Wisdom, intermeddle with all the delights of GOD, assume the similitude of his knowledge and goodness, make all his Works his Riches, his Laws his Delights, his Counsels his Contemplations, his Wayes his Joyes, and his Attributes his Perfections! He that appropriates all the World, and makes it his own peculiar is like unto GOD, meet to be his Son, and fit to live in Communion with him. The Kingdom of GOD is made visible to him to whom all Kingdoms are so many Mansions of Joy, and all Ages but the streets of his own City. The man that sees all Angels and Men his Fellow-members, and the whole Family of GOD in Heaven and Earth, his own Domesticks, is fit for Heaven. (*CE,* 276–77)

One of the most important effects of this dazzling profusion of words in repetitive, yet shifting patterns is to create an impression of the richness of infinity and thereby to bring the reader to "appropriate the world" by seeing all things as simultaneously, immediately, and intimately related. The language Traherne uses, in its incantatory repetitions, its naming of all the gifts of God, and its thrusting outward to the most inclusive, abstract perspective possible is an imitative and appropriate device for expressing that expansion as well as for inducing it in the reader. By calling the multifarious and glorious things of God and His Creation to mind so that the soul comprehends "all Kingdoms" and "all Ages," the soul loses its self-centeredness. It is so filled with riches that nothing is left for it to desire, and thus perceiving the sacred presence of God in the whole universe, the soul is not drawn away into selfishness and sin through deprivation but is sustained against all difficulties in heaven and earth.

This final fulfillment of the soul in transcending the limits of its own temporal ignorance is the subject of the third and last movement of the paragraph in which he virtually overwhelms the reader with examples of those things that stand ready to give the soul help, comfort, and support once its vision has been attained. In this list or naming of things that await the enlightened soul Traherne provides one of the longest and most intense examples of repetition to be found anywhere in his works. Like God's plenty pouring itself out in selfless abandon, the word *more* is repeated forty-two times in the space of twenty-eight lines, and the paragraph finally ends in a reassertion of the paradox that appropriating the world to oneself in the manner he recommends is not only unselfish and godlike but the source of fulfillment for all other souls as well. Again, we are asked to contemplate the mystery of a unity, a oneness, that is at the same time infinitely rich and full: "the Magazine and Store-house of all Perfection." The passage is long, but it must be seen whole for it to convey its full effect of massive repetition, the sense that, at the end, one has at last reached a height from which he is able to see all things at a glance—one and together in a continuum of inexhaustible plenitude. The paragraph continues from the last quotation:

As he hath more encouragements to believe in GOD, and to delight in him, so hath he more concerns to engage his fear, more allurements to provoke his desire, more incentives to enflame his love, and more obligations to compel his obedience: More arguments to strengthen his Hope, more materials to feed his Praises, more Causes to make him Humble, more fuel for Charity to others, more grounds of Contentment in himself, more helps to inspire him with Fortitude, more rewards to quicken his Industry, more engagements to Circumspection and Prudence, more ballast to make him Stable, more lights to assist his Knowledge, more sails to forward his Motion, more employments in which to spend his Time, more attractives to Meditation, and more entertainments to enrich his Solitude. He hath more aids to confirm his Patience, more avocations from Injuries to Meekness, more wings to carry him above the World, and more Gates to let him into Heaven. He hath more *Withholders* to keep him from Sin, more aggravations to increase his Guilt, more odious deformities in every Vice, more waters to augment his Tears, more motives to Repentance, and more Consolations upon his Reconciliation: More hopes to relieve his Prayer, more bounds to secure his Prosperity, more comforts in Adversity, and more Hallelujah's in all Estates: More delights to entertain his Friends, more sweetness in his Conversation, more arts to conquer his Enemies, more Feasts in abstemious Fasts, more and better sawce than other at his Feasts, innumerable Companions night and day, in Health, in Sickness, in Death, in Prison; at his Table, in his Bed, in his Grove, in his Garden, in the City, in the Field, in his Journy, in his Walk, at all times, and in all places. He hath more antidotes against Temptation, more weapons in his Spiritual Warfare, more balsom for his Wounds, and more preservatives against the contagion of Worldly Customs. From this Spring of *Universal Fruition* all the streams of Living Waters flow that refresh the Soul. Upon this Hing[e] all a mans Interests turn, and in this Centre all his Spiritual Occasions meet. It is the great Mystery of Blessedness and Glory, the Sphere of all Wisdom, Holiness and Piety, the great and ineffable Circumstance of all Grace and Vertue, the Magazine and Storehouse of all Perfection. (*CE,* 277)

The rhetoric of this passage accomplishes even more energetically what Fish has said is accomplished by Browne's rhetoric in the *Religio Medici,* the "resolving" of everything into God, except that one has no impression from Traherne that existing barriers and distinctions are being broken down or resolved. Rather, distinctions and barriers are being transcended and seen, not as destroyed (resolved) but as completely transformed in character by the expansion of the perceiving mind. For Traherne the distinctions (which are only appearances) are not resolved into pieces when their true reality is recognized. Instead, they are expanded or made infinite in extent and number because it is understood that they are at one and the same moment both God and simply what they appear to be. It is this deepest of all paradoxes that excites Traherne and toward which he directs all of his rhetoric of Gratitude.

Thus Traherne's language is not a "self-consuming artifact" in which the normal logic of statement is first presented then broken down, nor is it a "self-indulgent" one (like Browne's) in which attention is called to its own cleverness. Traherne's language is, however, self-transcendent, raising and expanding the self to infinity and eternity so that the whole universe can be included in it. Gratitude is ultimately "acknowledge-ment and benevolence united-together" (CE, 276), and its rhetoric is inclusive, rising to the highest of spiritual levels:

The Soul perhaps may be transformed to Gratitude, as Gratitude is to Contentment, and Praise, and Thanksgiving. But it will have no Body, no frail and corruptible Flesh, no bones or members to look after. All its operations are of one kind, all its works and concernments are the same. It has no Fear, or Care to divert it; no impediment, or danger, or distraction. Pure Gratitude is so divine a thing, that the Soul may safely wish to be turned *all* into Gratitude. (CE, 275–76)

To return, at last, to an earlier point: Traherne's language is essen-tially meditative, although the long paragraph we have been examining is obviously not an example of any formal meditation. There is no composition of place, no division into parts, and no ending colloquy with God, but in a deeper way the passage is permeated with the real purpose of meditation—the alteration of the mind or soul by a proper directing of its thoughts. The repetitive, abstract, and paradoxical rhetoric which arises from Traherne's pursuit of this objective consti-tutes his rhetoric of Gratitude, and it is a significant cause of a certain breathtaking quality in his prose, that strangely individual, yet imper-sonal sense of exhilaration we find in Traherne's language at its best. And in *Christian Ethicks* Traherne is often at his best, demonstrating a mastery of his characteristic rhetoric that is confident and mature, especially when he begins near the middle of the work to transcend the limitations of conventional moral idiom and to express his own perspective on the virtues and their place in the transformation of the soul. His prose then becomes a tool, designed and tempered for one purpose alone: to "adorn our souls with the Beauty of all objects whatsoever" so that they will be "transformed into the Image of GOD" (*CE*, 52).

# Chapter Three

# Meditations on the Six Days of the Creation

## Six Days and their Genesis

Until recently it was assumed that *Meditations on the Six Days of the Creation*[1] was an early work, composed, as Gladys Wade thought, sometime between 1661 and 1667.[2] Traherne's authorship had itself been questioned by Helen White and reestablished beyond reasonable doubt by Catherine Owen in 1961, but when in 1971 Richard Lynn Sauls discovered that Traherne had relied heavily upon a well-known work on meditation by the Jesuit Father Louis de la Puente "for ideas and phraseology as well as . . . overall structure,"[3] it was clear not only that the *Six Days* was not an early work but also why it might have been presumed both to be early and perhaps not by Traherne at all. As Sauls has shown, it is highly derivative, a little over half of its ninety-one pages "contain[ing] debts to Puente,"[4] and thus most of it is not in Traherne's characteristic style. There is, in fact, little or nothing in it that could be called the rhetoric of Gratitude so abundantly displayed in *Christian Ethicks.* Many of the themes and the ways of approaching them do not seem very much like Traherne's until the last few pages of the work, where Traherne relaxes his dependency upon Puente and begins to express himself in his own way.

The discovery that Traherne had borrowed heavily from Puente for the *Six Days* was accompanied in Saul's article by the further discovery that Traherne had taken almost as much from Puente for his "Church's Year-Book,"[5] a manuscript of "devotions on the principal days of the Church calendar from Easter to All Saints' Day."[6] This double borrowing from Puente furnished the chief link between these works and is one of the most significant indications that they were written very close to each other in time. There are, as well, a number of borrowings in both works from such devotional authors as Daniel Featley (1582–1645),

William Austin (1587–1634), Jeremy Taylor (1613–1667), and Lancelot Andrewes (1555–1626) that also help to establish the close proximity of composition, about which Sauls concludes:

Carol Marks has clearly shown that the Year-Book was written in 1670 (pp. 32–34). A study of Traherne's use of sources indicates that the Meditations [the *Six Days*], a work very similar in style, was composed near that date.[7]

That Traherne also borrowed from Puente for his *Thanksgivings* links that work in time with the *Six Days* and the "Year-Book" as well. Sauls, accepting the assumptions of earlier scholars, thinks the *Thanksgivings* was first in order of composition, asserting that Traherne discovered Puente "shortly before or at the time he wrote his first two Thanksgivings," and that he "put Puente's work aside" for the rest of the Thanksgivings but "took it up again when he came to write his *Meditations on the Six Days of the Creation.*"[8] However, it seems likely that Traherne would have used his source more fully at the beginning of his concern with it than later, moving from greater to lesser dependency. For this reason and because the *Thanksgivings* is in several intangible ways involved with more advanced rhetorical concerns, such as the development of an individual style, it is more reasonable to suppose that the *Thanksgivings* was last in order of composition, rather than first. The recent discoveries of Marks and Sauls, therefore, suggest a new chronology for these three works: first, the "Year-Book" (as Marks has demonstrated, written between April and November, 1670), then shortly after or at the same time, the *Six Days* (1670/71), and finally, the *Thanksgivings* (1671/72).

Another question remains, however: what were the motivations behind their composition? Carol Marks has tried to answer this question as it applies to the "Year-Book," and her speculations are also valid for both the *Six Days* and the *Thanksgivings.* After considering the possibility that Traherne intended the "Year-Book" for publication, for private devotion, or for the use of some other person, Marks concludes that "It seems in fact to embody something of all these possibilities, a composite production of Traherne as vicar, chaplain, private Christian, friend."[9] Such an embodiment is consistent, also, with the idea that all three works may have been undertaken as a kind of apprenticeship to Traherne's new position in the Bridgeman household, a more sophisticated environment than he had known in Credenhill. Perhaps he decided to rededicate and prepare himself anew by turning to the practice of a more public and institutional form of devotion than his "Select Meditations" (ca.1665) represented, which might have been all that he had written before he moved to London.[10] If so, the "Year-Book" and the *Six Days* would be the first attempts to adapt himself to a new, broader audience, and the *Thanksgivings* something of a culmination of these efforts, a work wherein he finds his own voice.

## Traherne's Use of Puente

Whatever the final truth may be about the order or purpose of composition of these three works, except for several borrowed passages early on, Traherne used the beginning pages of Puente's work as a general guide for the meditational structure in which he wrote the first few of his Thanksgivings. But for his *Meditations on the Six Days of the Creation* he turned to the last part of Puente's second volume where he found, ready-made, a group of meditations on the Creation. These meditations and Puente's whole work have their sources in the mystical tradition descending from Dionysius the Areopagite through St. Bernard (1091–1153), the Victorines (later twelfth century), and St. Bonaventure (1221–1274). The work's organization is based upon the three stages of the mystical way: Purgative, Illuminative, and Unitive, each being further subdivided into two parts, making a "six-branched tree" like Bonaventure's six wings in the *Itinerarium Mentis in Deum* (1259). The material with which Traherne chose to deal was meant for those who are concerned with the Unitive way. As Puente expresses it,

Those which treate of union in the Unitive life, shall finde meditations of the Seven divine Attributes, wherein principally this union is fed; that is to say: Bountie, Charitie, Mercie, Immensitie, Wisdome, Omnipotencie, and Providence. And if they will meditate God's benefits, they shall find meditations of the workes that almightie God did the first sixe dayes of the worlde, and his rest upon the seventh day.[11]

Beyond finding Puente's meditations on the Creation attractive because they are directed toward spiritual ends, Traherne would also have found them especially suited to one who was either beginning or trying to become more proficient in the practice of meditation. Puente's design in writing them was many-sided, and he was both clear and direct in explaining that readers were to appropriate them as they wished in order to meet their own spiritual needs. His directions for their use describe exactly what Traherne did in adapting them to his own purposes. After suggesting that the reader should expand or condense each meditative point as he finds it appropriate to himself, Puente gives him free reign with the language as well:

Yet it is to bee noted, that although wee prescribe in them the practize of mentall praier, exercizing affections, petitions, and colloquies, yet tye wee no man to those wordes wherein they are delivered, but hee himselfe may invent them, as our Lord shall dictate the same unto him, & the light of the veritie which hee considereth, and his owne feeling of devotion, the which. . . is the tongue of the soule: and whosoever hath it, knoweth very well how to speake with almighty God, and without it, is as it were mute and dumbe: and then it is good to make use of those colloquies heere set downe, making them as if they were his owne.[12]

A few lines later Puente is still more generous in offering his material to those writing "sermons, or spiritual speeches," an offer that not only helps to explain further Traherne's extensive and unacknowledged borrowing in the present case but also to indicate a general awareness that religious and devotional writings, like the words of the Bible, were shared experiences, belonging to and used by all as they saw fit, not (insofar as they were true expressions of the spirit) the property of any single person. Puente's generosity, then, as well as Traherne's acceptance of it, is not an expression of an individual personality trait but a manifestation of a common spiritual bond shared by all who participated in the spirit. We have in this fact another and complementary way of understanding Traherne's tendency toward what Stewart describes as an "open form," a sense of participation with the reader in the process of composition. As Puente's words suggest, that tendency is itself part of the spiritual tradition in which Traherne understood himself to be participating. Puente is here speaking specifically of those in monasteries or other religious houses, but the same sense of sharing in a common verbal expression of spiritual meaning was felt across the boundaries of Catholic and Protestant, layman and priest. Puente writes,

And besides this, they may also helpe themselves herewithall for their owne sermons, or spirituall speeches, which are used to be made in common to such as live in religion, or out of the same, with desire to obtaine that perfection that is proper to their estate.[13]

In appropriating Puente as he does, Traherne is not only learning and practicing the art of meditation but also fulfilling his role as preserver of and participant in a tradition of shared spiritual awareness.

## Puente, Traherne, and the Hexameral Tradition

In using Puente's meditations on the Creation, Traherne is also participating, although indirectly, in a very old and once popular tradition of writing commentaries on the account in Genesis of God's work in creating the world. These commentaries on the six days of God's labor *(hexamera)* had begun at least as early as Philo Judaeus (c.25 B.C.–50 A.D.) and had developed over the centuries into sometimes highly elaborate exercises involving a wide range of materials drawn from philosophy, theology, legend, and natural history, purporting to teach a variety of moral, practical, and spiritual lessons. Until the mid-seventeenth century it was generally assumed by writers in the hexameral tradition—and there were a great many—that the scriptural account of the Creation provided exact scientific knowledge, though veiled, about plants, animals, geological phenomena, and atmospheric conditions. This same assumption lies behind the customary practice of beginning every history, of whatever time and nation, with an account of the Creation, as Sir Walter Ralegh (1552?–1618) does in his *History of the World* (1614), for example, and it is responsible for such *hexamera* as *The Divine Weeks and Works* (1578) of Guiliaume DuBartas (1544–1590) in Joshua Sylvester's (1563–1618) immensely popular translation (1605), where a semiscientific interest is combined with highly imaginative and literary concepts. Although other *hexamera* of the sixteenth and early seventeenth centuries were not as creatively conceived nor as popular as Sylvester's translation of DuBartas, most of them did share with it the same quality of putting natural history, theology, literature, and piety together into a general mixture. Such works as Lambert Daneau's (1530–1595/96) *Wonderful Workmanship of the World* (1578) and Henry Ainsworth's (1571–1622/23) *Annotations Upon the First Book of Moses, Called Genesis* (1616) are in different ways examples of this tendency to include all levels of thought and reference in a single perspective.

But the tradition of mixing science and spirituality was nearly over before the middle of the century. Under the more rigid scrutiny of newly developing tests of truth, writers of *hexamera* could not so freely assume that the Bible's science and the received facts about animals and their behavior were such fully valid expressions of reality as they had been thought to be. After John Swan's (fl. 1635) well-known *Speculum Mundi* (1635), *hexamera* changed their character as writers began to confine themselves more and more to reading Genesis simply as a source of religious and moral ideas. The great compilations of hexameral lore by the Calvinist David Pareus (1609) and the Jesuit Benedictus Pererius (1601), both of which Swan drew upon, were losing most of their authority, and to explore Genesis in the old way was not an acceptable means of gaining information about the causes of natural phenomena, the habits of animals, or the geographical location of paradise. As Arnold Williams tells us,

Poets no longer turned to Pererius or Pareus for information on how the heavens and earth rose out of chaos, nor did the historians begin their works at the creation of the world. Genesis subsided into a religious document solely. Commentators lost the art of wrapping up literature, science, history, mythology, and devotion into one bundle; and so the commentary on Genesis as it had been known in the sixteenth and early seventeenth century ceased.[14]

Traherne, writing as late as 1670, would hardly have turned to the hexameral tradition for its scientific learning, and in Puente he found the perspective that suited his own. As we have already seen, Puente's concern is with the religious, moral meaning of the Creation as a basis for meditation, even though he wrote his work before the decline of the earlier hexameral style. He follows many of the traditional notions about the divisions of God's labor, the three sorts of beasts created, and the meaning of light, but Puente treats these matters as the basis of moral and spiritual edification only. Before Puente begins his meditations on the Creation, he asserts that he does not intend to handle any of the scientific, historical, or legendary material often treated in other *hexamera,* "because for the scope of these meditations, it importeth little to knowe the same."[15] Traherne was in full agreement with this approach.

## Traherne's Adaptations

Traherne's use does not change the scope of Puente's meditations but stays very close to their intention and structure, following Puente's points and instructions about them with the kind of fidelity we would expect of one involved in learning the art of meditation through imitating, personalizing, and reshaping the material provided for general use—as Puente's was. For example, because Puente's work is a manual written to instruct the reader in meditation and to present samples during the process of instruction, he uses the first person: "In this consideration I may discourse through the quires of Angels," he remarks, suggesting that the reader should follow the same practice. Puente speaks directly in the role of the meditating soul only in the interspersed colloquies he provides as examples after he has announced the particular subject of each meditation and divided it into separately numbered points.

Characteristically, Traherne does not keep Puente's formal division between points nor his individual meditative sections but runs them into each other by means of transitional paragraphs so that each day's meditations constitute an integrated movement of mental prayer with a colloquy in the form of a poem at the end. Also, but in accordance with Puente's intentions, Traherne alters Puente's tone by presenting the meditative voice as one immediately involved in considering the meanings of each day's work and admonishing his own soul to call upon God for illumination and grace. Traherne is direct and dramatic; instead of being told how meditation is performed, we are witnesses to a soul engaged, and we follow its various movements as our own. Traherne is transforming a handbook suggestion into specific practice, and he follows the handbook's meditative points in their order but shortens some and skips over others, moving across and softening their sharp divisions into a more unified, uninterrupted expression of the soul in meditation. He also gives a new kind of unity to the whole work by beginning each day's meditation (except the second) with the words from Psalm 19 ("Let the words of my mouth, and the meditation of my heart, be acceptable in thy sight, O Lord"). For this, as well as for ending each day's meditation with a poem, he may be indebted to William Austin's *Devotionis Augustinianae Flamma* (1635).[16]

As a means of indicating how he uses Puente, we may look at Traherne's First Day's Meditation, where, after making Puente's opening more precise and direct, he treats Puente's brief reference to Isaiah 40:12 as specific instruction and expands it by quoting the whole verse and adapting it to the voice of the soul in meditation. Isaiah's question, "Who hath measured the waters in the hollow of his hand," Traherne changes to a direct address to God: "Thou hast measured . . . thou hast meted." Then, following Puente's acceptance of the Augustinian notion that the angels were created with the first light, Traherne begins his own meditation upon the meaning of this creation of light, changing Puente's "First is to be considered"[17] into "Consider, O my Soul" and composing lines of his own interspersed with a few adaptations of Puente's phrases.

Traherne proceeds on his own for a number of pages, meditating upon the fall of certain of these angels and considering why God allowed such a thing to happen:

But why, O Lord, didst thou suffer these glorious Spirits to apostatize and fall from thee? Was it not to teach us, that none were in their own Natures perfect, but only thou alone, most holy and ever blessed God? (*Six Days,* 3)

The reasons he first suggests are found to be insufficient, until he explains (as he also does in the *Ethicks*) that it is because God's creatures must be free to perfect their virtues and come to love God by their own will. Constraint would destroy the whole meaning of love, and love is the only principle that gives significance to virtue:

But Glory ariseth from an interior Excellency of a Being, and by inward Perfections only to be attained. That therefore they might be holy and wise themselves, which is glorious, thou didst permit them either to stand or fall;

not at all desiring they should fall, but that by their own Choice, they might
stand more perfectly in their Bliss and Glory. (*Six Days*, 6)

All of this Traherne has elaborated from a brief statement by Puente
about the creation of the angels in a perfect state.

The subject of Traherne's next meditative section, concerning the
guardian angels that watch over and help man, was probably taken
from Daniel Featley's *Ancilla Pietatis* (1626),[18] but in the next page
Traherne returns to Puente's *Meditations* and carries out his instructions
by praising God when Puente says to praise and by considering what
Puente says to consider.

Traherne continues in this same fashion until the last six or seven
pages of the *Six Days*, taking up Puente's points in order, cutting out
phrases and sections, making the language direct and immediate and
expanding upon Puente's instructions. An excellent demonstration of
Traherne's method throughout can be found in his adaption of Puente's
third point. It is one of the most interesting and illuminating of
Traherne's transformations of Puente, and it can be understood best,
perhaps, by setting down Puente and Traherne line by line, with
Puente's words in italics directly above those of Traherne's:

*Thirdly is to be considered, how the earth at*
Consider, O my Soul, how this Earth at

*this instant was void and emptie, and darknes*
the first Instant of Creation was void and empty, and that *Darknes*

*was over the face of the depth: so that all the*
did cover the Face thereof.

*distance which there was betwixt heaven, and earth, whether it were water, cloud, or*
*ayre, all was darknes, and without light.*
*1. Wherein is to be pondered first, the imperfection, which at that present, both earth*
*and the water had, for the earth was as void and emptie, without attaining the*
*proper end of its Creation, void of trees, and of inhabitants, and all was in*
*darknes, for lack of light. If therfore the earth and*
                                                Think if it

*the water, had had understanding, and a toung,*
could                          have                    spoke,

*they would have cryed out to their Creator,*
how earnestly it would have cried out

*craving the perfection which was wanting to them.*
for that Light                    it                    wanted.
Consider how void and empty it was indeed, having neither Trees nor
    Inhabitants; and in this Light see the Wisdom, Goodness, and Power of
    Almighty God in sending all, and praise him for all.

*In all which I may consider my selfe, a man*
In this Light also look upon thine own self.

*earthly, and miserable,*
A Person earthly, miserable, void, and empty,

*conceaved in sinne, by the sinne*
conceived in Sin, destitute, by the Fall

*of Adam; who therfore in the beginning*
of *Adam*, of the End to which thou wert

*of my being, was void and emptie, destitute of the end for which I was created, void*
first                                                        created and void

*of grace, and of virtues, and covered*
of Grace    and    Virtue,    covered

*all over with the horrible darknes*
all over with Sin and Darkness; (*Six Days*, 10–11)

*of ignorance and sinne: (Puente, 2:711)*

The most striking change Traherne makes here is in the direction of
the speaking voice. As Puente expected of his readers, Traherne turns
Puente's instructional perspective into a personal one, addressing his
own soul and urging it to consider, think, and feel in the active process
of meditation. But in adapting it to the speaking voice of the meditating soul, Traherne also condenses and transposes Puente's phrases. His
reduction of Puente's indirect "If therfore the earth and the water, had
had understanding, and a toung . . ." to a direct expression of the
heart. "Think if it could have spoke, how earnestly it would have cried
out . . .," is typical and effective. The transpositions of phrases
Traherne makes ("void and empty" and "destitute of the end," for

example) are made for the same fundamental purpose of increasing the immediacy of the meditating voice.

But we see another, and significant, change Traherne brings about in Puente's material. Although that change in this short passage is slight, throughout the work as a whole and particularly toward its end, this sort of revision has a considerable cumulative effect. Among all the words about the imperfections and miserableness of both earth and man, Traherne adds a distinctive note of optimism and cause for joy. Following Puente's language, Traherne first "Consider[s] how void and empty it [the world] was indeed," but then adds a clause of his own: "in this Light see the Wisdom, Goodness, and Power of Almighty God in sending all, and praise him for all." This optimistic note is one of the chief means by which Traherne makes his adaptation of Puente into something more than an exercise in appropriating another author's material. Puente's work is not itself dark or melancholy, but it is less joyful and optimistic than Traherne's, especially toward its end wherein Traherne writes five pages of prose and two of poetry without any direct dependence upon Puente.

Like Traherne, Puente has a high regard for man as the epitome of the Creation (an attitude that owes something to the hexameral tradition and Renaissance Christian humanism) and emphasizes the soul's nature as the image of God—its mirroring of the Trinity in Understanding, Will, and Memory, and its infinite capacity to contain all things. Puente writes:

The third [point] shall be to consider, how almightie God, three and one, created man to his image and likenes, giving him a soule (wherin principally this image consisteth) like to himselfe in the supreamest degree of intellectuall Being, and in the most excellent perfections of the divinity which can be communicated to creatures.[19]

And from this statement he elaborates six "excellencies" of the soul wherein "it is the image of God": (1) its pure spirituality, (2) its immortality and separateness from the world, (3) its three faculties of Understanding, Memory, and Will, (4) its freedom, (5) its infinite capacity to receive all blessedness, virtue, and knowledge, and finally, (6) its superiority to all things, since it is "the last end wherto they are ordayned." These are Traherne's own beliefs, and he continues to adapt Puente's words through these points, though with greater freedom to alter than he exercised at the beginning of his adaptation. But after this Traherne does not use Puente's language further. Instead, he begins to bring his own work to a close by summing up what has gone before and engaging in a long series of praises to God for all His gifts to man:

By these you may see what manner of Man he ought to be, and what manner of Life he ought to lead. For being the End of the World, and the Image of God, for whose Sake the World was made, his Life must be spent in enjoying that which was made for him, and in praising God for that which he enjoyeth. (*Six Days,* 85)

Puente, on the other hand, continues with the details of the creation of Adam and Eve, the naming of beasts, and the dominion of Adam over them, with reflections upon the frailty of the clay from which man was fashioned and the passions to which he is subject. Although Puente's reflections overall are not pessimistic, they tend to remind man of his subordinate, humble position:

Finally to flye all sinnes, I will remember, that it is they which breake and dissolve this worke of clay, and convert the same into the dust, wherof it was made, conforme to the sentence which God our Lord gave against Adam, saying. That he should, returne to earth, of which he was taken.[20]

Traherne prefers to concentrate upon the resurrection, and after several pages of praise: "O thou inexhausted, undrainable Ocean of everlasting Goodness, I praise thee for communicating unto us thine incommunicable Attributes . . ." (*Six Days,* 88), he ends the work on a high note of joy which contrasts sharply with Puente's reminder that the body is dust and will to dust return:

That Body is the living Vessel of eternal Glory, into which Love shall pour forth all its Emanations, in which it shall act and exercise, and which it shall ever ravish by the Sweetness of its Operations . . . So that Angels and Men are its Treasures, and God for loving Angels and Men, and all Creatures that dignify them; all these Joys concentring in it, ravish the Body with most grateful Motions, and stir the Spirit with the sweetest Touches that even Love it self can inspire into pleased and happy Souls. (*Six Days,* 89)

In spite of the fact that the *Six Days* is an exercise in the art of meditation, it gives the general impression of originality. Traherne has managed to place upon it the impress of his own personal style. He has added a new unity to the work, and by transforming Puente's instructional perspective into the direct voice of the meditating soul he has given to the *Six Days* an interesting dramatic quality. In doing so, he has also occasionally exhibited some of that paralleling, repetitive rhetoric that is used to great effect in the *Ethicks.* In the *Six Days,* however, that rhetoric remains in a rudimentary form, with little integration into other basic structures, as in the last few pages wherein he writes a series of sixteen sentences (beginning with the phrase "I praise thee. . .") which are not constructed with any special care and simply sum up the gifts of the Creation for which man is to give thanks to God. Traherne possessed the ability to express himself effectively, but for the most part he seems in the *Six Days* to ignore his own potential. It is not until the *Thanksgivings* that he begins to experiment and develop those structures that are such a marked feature of his later prose.

# Chapter Four
## Thanksgivings

The collection of nine meditations first published in 1699 as *A Serious and Pathetical Contemplation of the Mercies of God, in Several Most Devout and Sublime Thanksgivings for the Same* is a work deserving more attention than it has received. Stanley Stewart called it a "marvelous little work,"[1] but he did not find a place in his own study of Traherne to do more than note the closeness with which the language of these Thanksgivings imitates that of the Psalms. There is truth in the assertion of Harold Fisch who has said that the Thanksgivings are, "in some passages, little more than a pastiche of Psalm-poetry,"[2] but the work as a whole is much more than that.

It may be that Traherne's attempt to blend his voice with that of David's whom he and others in the century called the "sweet singer of Israel,"[3] has tended to distract the attention of critics from other merits of the composition. Traherne does use long passages from the Psalms and other books of the Bible as though they were his own, and he reconstructs their cadences and diction even when the words themselves *are* his own, but how much or how skillfully he imitates David or any devotional writer is not finally what makes the *Thanksgivings* important to a study of Traherne. What is important is that in the *Thanksgivings* Traherne engages in a stylistic and structural experimentation in which one can observe him in the process of developing his paralleling, repetitive style. Not only does he make use of and alter the traditional Ignatian structure to suit his own purposes but, perhaps through the influence of Daniel Featley, he also explores the possibilities of the device of clustered or bracketed words and phrases deriving largely from the *Private Devotions* (1648) of Lancelot Andrewes. In the *Thanksgivings* one can see the bracketing and paralleling of structures maturing from an awkward, mechanical technique into a smoothly functional device that is expressive of Traherne's distinct spiritual perspective.

Unfortunately, there is no extant manuscript of the *Thanksgivings,* and we are not certain exactly what Traherne himself intended the work to be, whether it is a completed whole as we have it or whether some part of it was added to either by Rev. George Hickes (its first publisher) or by Mrs. Hopton. A general ordering of ideas that is similar to the patterns in the Burney manuscript of poems and the *Centuries of Meditations,* as well as a linking of most of the Thanksgivings in sequence by reference back to the one immediately preceding suggest, however, that with the possible exception of the last Thanksgiving the work was conceived as an integrated unit,[4] even though it is possible that it is only a fragment of what Traherne had planned originally.

Whether it is a fragment or not, the work displays a diversity in style which seems to indicate that Traherne was deliberately experimenting with line lengths and bracketing devices and that he wrote the *Thanksgivings* over several years' time in which his style matured. Gladys Wade thought all of the Thanksgivings were written before 1665–66, but recent scholarship has indicated that they were not begun before 1665 and, as we have seen, probably not even before 1670. Very likely the last one was not written until sometime in the period between 1672 and 1674. This last, or ninth, Thanksgiving is, in fact, different from the others in both subject and tone. Instead of continuing on a metaphysical level to treat of God's works, blessings, and attributes, the "Thanksgiving and Prayer for the Nation" turns to the more concrete problems of country and people, lamenting their sins and praying for their deliverance from the sufferings of war and other tribulations. This change in tone and content, the apparent sincerity of it, as well as its stylistic shift, all suggest that the last Thanksgiving was composed sometime during England's involvement in the Third Dutch War (1672–74), perhaps even as a response to Orlando Bridgeman's disagreement with Charles II's secret politics related to that war and Bridgeman's removal (1672) as Keeper of the Great Seal. If these speculations are correct (and they seem to account more convincingly than any others for the character of the last Thanksgiving), they would further suggest that not only do the Thanksgivings constitute a group of eight rather than nine meditative units but also that in the ninth, "unintegrated" meditation we have a more mature example of the style Traherne was working toward in the earlier ones.

If the *Thanksgivings* is a kind of "workshop" in which Traherne was forging his most characteristic devices, then its various techniques provide a basis for comparison between various levels of success and also some insight into what are significant sources of his style. In addition the Thanksgivings give us a remarkable look at Traherne's approach to the tradition of formal Ignatian meditation, for he followed at the beginning of the work a strict meditational structure but gradually moved away from it into freer and less restrictive patterns. Finally, the *Thanksgivings* and the *Meditations on the Six Days of the Creation* are the only exceptions to Francis King's otherwise correct observation that Traherne does not write as though he were immediately involved in the act of meditation itself, that is, of actively searching for the ultimate vision. In the *Thanksgivings* Traherne writes, as he does in the *Six Days,* from the perspective of the "I" who meditates, a position which he will rarely take in other work. This fact may be an additional indication that the *Thanksgivings* is an earlier experimental work written close to the *Six Days* in both time and purpose.

## Meditational Backgrounds

Traherne's purpose in all he wrote was meditational in that he sought always to establish for himself and others the perception of God as the infinite, eternal reality in and behind all things. In the later works such as *Christian Ethicks* this purpose led him to write a reiterative, incantatory style that reflects the deep levels of movement undergone by the mind as it makes its way toward the contemplative vision. In the *Thanksgivings* it is possible to see Traherne, through experimentation with line lengths and various patterns of repetition, moving in the direction of that style in which he was to write the *Centuries* and the *Ethicks*, the repetition of parallel structures in a dazzling variety of forms from single words to intricate phrases, sentences, and even larger sections of paragraphs. In the first few Thanksgivings this piling up of words and phrases in synonymous stacks or strings is frequently perfunctory, but in the later Thanksgivings it becomes a flexible device well integrated into the context.

At the same time that Traherne is experimenting with these devices he is reshaping the more formal structure of the Ignatian meditative exercise into a longer, looser unit in which few if any divisions between sections remain. Traherne begins the *Thanksgivings* with a close adherence to the Ignatian meditation, as it was recommended by Puente.

According to this Ignatian pattern, as Louis Martz explains, a "formal meditation" will usually fall "into three distinguishable portions, corresponding to the acts of memory, understanding, and will— portions which we might call composition, analysis, and colloquy."[5] These portions may frequently involve a "premeditation" in the composition section, in which the subject to be developed is, as Puente puts it, "first prepared, well digested, and divided into pointes."[6] Then the analysis may proceed in two or more subdivisions, exploring the subject in a variety of ways until the spiritual principles derived from it are, in the colloquy section of the meditation, accepted by the will and integrated into the soul. In the prescription of St. Ignatius, the final colloquy section is supposed to end with an actual colloquy or prayer, as Martz explains, "and may be addressed to the Father, or to the Son, or to the Virgin—or to all in sequence."[7]

Both the spirit of the Ignatian meditation and the form it is to take are well suggested by Puente's description of its procedure, and Puente's statements strongly suggest the tone and structure of Traherne's first several Thanksgivings. Outlining the three major divisions, Puente says the person meditating is

1. . . . with the memory to be mindefull of God our Lorde, with whom wee are to speake, and to negociate; and to be mindefull also of the mysterie that is to bee meditated, passing briefely thorough the memorie, with clearnesse, & distinction, that which is to be the matter of the meditation. . . .

2. . . . with the understanding to make severall discourses, and considerations about that mysterie, inquyring, and searching out the Verities comprehended therein, with all the causes, proprieties, effectes, and circumstances that it hath, pondering them very particularly. In such sort that the Understanding may forme a true, proper, and entire conceipt of the thing that it meditateth and may remain convinced, and perswaded to receive, and to embrace those truthes that it hath meditated, to propound them to the Will, and to move it therby to exercize its Actions.

3. . . . with the freedom of our will to draw forth sundry Affections, or vertuous Actes, conformable to that which the Understanding hath meditated . . . as are Hatred of our selves; Sorrowe for our Sinnes; Confusion of our owne misery; Love of God; trust in his mercye; prayses of God; thanksgiving for benefits received; desire to obtaine true vertues. . . . resignation of our selves to the Will of God.[8]

That Traherne began the *Thanksgivings* by consciously following Puente amounts to almost a certainty. Aside from the fact that Puente's words here are strongly suggestive of what Traherne actually does, at about the time these Thanksgivings were being written Traherne was, as we know, extensively using Puente for the *Six Days* and the "Year Book." In addition, the two colloquies at the end of the first Thanksgiving are largely copied out of Puente. Having begun with a close adherence to the spirit and form of Puente's Ignatian structure, however, Traherne soon moves away from a strict imitation of its formal meditative patterns.

The *Thanksgivings* as a kind of laboratory for the development of Traherne's style has not previously been noticed, but it becomes clear once one has looked beyond the Psalm-like language in which the work is written. In the first two Thanksgivings Traherne is adopting and molding the Psalms into full Ignatian exercises. Having with the second Thanksgiving written a successfully formed Ignatian meditation, Traherne begins to make various changes in the basic structure until in the ninth Thanksgiving he has found a form that seems to suit him best: a long, unbroken colloquy with God that modulates from pessimism and darkness to joy and light.

## The Structure of Thanksgiving

The first Thanksgiving ("Thanksgivings for the Body") begins its composition of place (or preparation of the mind), calling upon the memory "to be mindefull of God our Lorde, with whom wee are to speake," by reciting five verses from Psalm 103: "Bless the Lord, O my Soul: and all that is within me bless his holy name." It moves by clear stages of mental preparation from intention ("My desire is, to praise thee") to determination ("I will praise thee") presenting for premeditation (using Psalm 139: 14–18) what is to be meditated upon: "My substance was not hid from thee when I was made in secret." The composition of place ends with line 32 in a further brief expression of praise, having thoroughly blended the language of the Psalms with its own:

> When I awake I am still with thee.
> Blessed be thy holy Name,
> O Lord, my God! (30–32)[9]

After this composition of place Traherne begins a three-part analysis
that seeks to develop in the understanding a thorough grasp of the
meditative subject by "inquyring, and searching out the Verities
comprehended therein." The first part of the analysis is devoted to
describing first generally, then specifically, the parts and functions that
demonstrate how wonderfully made the body is:

> Thou hast given me a Body,
> Wherein the glory of thy Power shineth,
> Wonderfully composed above the Beasts,
> Within distinguished into useful parts,
> Beautified without with many Ornaments.
>   Limbs rarely poised,
>                 And made for Heaven. (43–49)

Thus, the body is "A Treasury of Wonders" (61), and he explores this
idea for over a hundred lines in metrically varied phrases, elaborating
upon and detailing the excellence of those wonders that are to be found
in eyes, ears, nose, and tongue, moving from the description of specific
parts of the body to the general principles that lie behind those parts,
and from there to the inward perceptive power that informs and
coordinates these operations and "makes our centre equal to the
Heavens" (134).

   He begins the second part of the analysis (161) by inquiring as to the
causes of the physical world itself, asking why such things as bodies
were made at all:

> And why, O Lord, wouldst thou so delight
> To magnify the dust taken from the ground?
>   From the dark obscurity of a silent Grave
> Thou raisest it, O Lord! (161–64)

The elaboration of his Christian-Platonist answer becomes the subject
of the second part of the analysis, which continues for the next 180
lines:

> Thou hast hidden thy self
>         By an infinite miracle,
>             And made this World the Chamber of thy presence; the

ground and theatre of thy righteous Kingdom.
>    That putting us at a distance
>         A little from thee,
>    Thou mayest satisfie the Capacities
>         Of thy righteous Nature. (178–85)

Thus, because God's righteousness and glory cannot be manifested unless some other exists, we are made as that other to which righteousness can be communicated and thereby actualized.

In his further "inquyring and searching out" of truths to present to the understanding, Traherne gives a second answer to the same question, this time asserting that bodies were created simply as ends in themselves, to which other things are to minister. From this exalted position of the body Traherne shifts to one of his favorite themes, the greater significance of the soul: "My Body is but the Cabinet, or Case of my Soul:/What then, O Lord, shall the Jewel be!" (272–73); and then he meditates upon another favorite idea, which we have seen in the *Ethicks,* that the presence of other souls enhances the enjoyment of any single one. This second part of the analysis next develops the idea that we are exalted by the body because it is the means by which we are able to receive God's gift of the world to us, which gift is, as he points out in a short poem, the end for which the Creation has been manifested:

*O what Profoundness in my Body lies,*
*For whom the Earth was made, the Sea, the Skies!*
*So greatly high our humane Bodies are,*
*That Angels scarcely may with these compare.* (327–30)

The third part of the analysis section, which begins with line 342, continues with its searching of the understanding by repeating the thought "That every one's Glory is beneficial unto all; and every one/magnified in his place by Service" (347–48). The angels provide him with the main meditative point in this third part of the analysis, and he expresses the startling notion that the angels feel, see, and taste the glories of the physical universe through the bodies of men:

Thou makest us treasures
>         And joys unto them;
Objects of Delight, and spiritual Lamps,
>    Whereby they discern visible things. (395–98)

That angels obtain enjoyment of the world through the bodies of men leads to a consideration of the mysterious connection between the body and the spirit. That men are "lamps" by which the angels see the physical world means that our bodies are exalted and made glorious by the angels much as they will be made at the Resurrection. Such a glorification of the body has its basis in the existence of a continuous flow or circulation between body and soul wherein the joys the body feels through its senses flow out to the soul and are then returned to the body in a more exalted form. But in addition to this "spiritualizing" of joy and returning it to the body in higher form, the soul has its own independent influence. It communicates the divine attributes themselves—"His Goodness, Wisdom, Power, Love divine"—directly to the body and makes the body a worthy temple for God to dwell in. Because the body is a container for God Himself, it is a more exalted thing even than the sun, for the sun we see in the sky is, by contrast, a purely material thing (though it may aptly symbolize God) and in itself devoid of the life that is in the human body.

In the third and final movement of the analysis section (341–465), Traherne expresses the mutual interaction and effect of soul and body upon each other. The senses are the means by which the soul and the angels see in this world, and these senses inflame the soul with what they perceive. The soul, in her turn, ravishes the body with her own perception of "the Godheads glorious Excellence."

He begins the last section of the meditation, in which the subject is treated in relation to the will or affections, by confessing himself a sinner and humbling himself before God (466), and in doing so he seems once again to be directly following Puente, who prescribes "Hatred of our selves; Sorrowe for our Sinnes' . . . Love of God; trust in his mercye; . . . [and] resignation of our selves to the Will of God." Traherne, following the pattern, accuses himself of sins, but those he mentions seem hardly applicable to him either by temperament or by opportunity:

But now, O lord, how highly great have my Transgressions been, who have abused this thy glorious Creature, by Surfeiting and Excess, by Lust and Wantonness, by Drunkenness, by Passion, by immoderate Cares, excessive Desires, and earthly Fears? (466–70)

He modifies them, however, by adding, more pertinently, the sins of being too much involved in the world and engaging in "vain Conversation." After this self-abasement he asks God to help and sustain him so that he may accomplish his good intentions:

> Turn away mine Eyes
> From beholding Vanity.
> Enable me to wash my hands in Innocency.
> That I may compass thine altar about,
> And lift up my Hands
> To thy Holy Oracle. (484–89)

Finally, as further inspiration to the will, Traherne quotes a long passage from the Song of Songs and ends the first Thanksgiving with two short prayers or colloquies, which are based largely upon Puente, the first of which is distinctly reminiscent of the *Confessions* of St. Augustine. Traherne writes:

> *O Infinite God, Center of my Soul, Convert me powerfully unto thee,*
> *that in thee I may take Rest, for thou didst make me for thee, and my*
> *heart's unquiet till it be united to thee.* (526–28)

The second Thanksgiving ("Thansgivings for the Soul") is built even more closely upon the Ignatian structure and with even greater success: it contains a carefully integrated composition of place (1–61), a two-part analysis (62–313; 314–464), this time unbroken by verse, and an application of the meditation to the will (465–79) with its preliminary admission of sinfulness (480–535) followed by a concluding prayer (536–47). In this second Thanksgiving the movement is smooth and economical and there are no sudden shifts to break up the flow of thought and feeling. The two Thanksgivings are also linked sequentially by words and phrases near the beginning of the second that return to the thought of the first Thanksgiving and extend it, amplifying and contrasting it with the new meditational ideas. The first Thanksgiving moves toward a recognition of the deadness of the material world considered in itself and an admission that the body is nothing in comparison to the soul, which is the jewel held by the body (its case), and the second Thanksgiving begins with this same idea. After the

opening passages from Psalm 89, which prepare the mind for meditation, Traherne links the two Thanksgivings together by a clear reference to the first one that emphasizes the greater significance of the new
theme concerning the soul:

O Lord I rejoyce, and am exceeding glad;
       Because of thy Goodness,
In ⎧ Creating the World.
   ⎨ Giving Brightness to the Sun.
   ⎨ Ruling the Sea.
   ⎩ Framing the Limbs and Members of my Body.
But much more abundantly,
  For the Glory of my Soul. (9–16)

And he continues to elaborate upon the nature of the soul and its
powers. Now, however, there is an alteration in the tone and a corresponding difference in the verbal structures. The general sense of
excitement and expansiveness is higher, and as he turns to the active,
vital powers of the soul, he piles up parallel phrases, each beginning
with the same verb form so that the verb is given a heavy emphasis like
the tolling of a bell:

O my God!
  In the contemplation of my Soul
  I see the Truth of all Religion,
  Behold all the Mysteries of Blessedness,
  Admire thy Greatness,
  Rejoyce in thy Goodness,
  Praise thy Power,
  Adore thy Love,
  Am ravished with thy Wisdom,
  Transported,
  Pleased with the beauty of thy Holiness. (294–304)

Thus in this second Thanksgiving Traherne experiments with the
repetition of parallel structures. Such repetitions are closer together
than in the first Thanksgiving, and they circle first around one word or
part of speech and then around another in a variety of patterns.

This second, or "Thanksgivings for the Soul," is the most coherent example of meditative structure in all the *Thanksgivings*. Even though in a general way Traherne follows the Ignatian pattern in all of the first four, that pattern is interrupted by several poems in the first Thanksgiving and begins to lose its structural clarity in the third. In the second, however, Traherne composes a clear Ignatian structure, with well-defined divisions between the parts.

In the third, "Thanksgivings for the Glory of God's Works," the divisions become less clear. Indeed, the next few Thanksgivings are not marked by any obviously progressive movement toward a new meditative structure, but the number of meditative sections is reduced so that there arises instead one essentially long movement in two closely integrated phases, a negative unregenerate and searching phase which turns gradually to one that is positive, triumphant, and joyful. Thanksgivings five and six contain a noticeable blending of sections into a longer movement, and in Thanksgiving seven there is an obvious division of the analysis section into two broad phases, one of searching for a book that would assure the soul of God's purposes and a second one of joyfulness at having found the Bible wherein the whole magnificent story of the Creation is set forth.

In the seventh Thanksgiving Traherne provides no sharp divisions between a composition of place and analysis section, but he does take up first a description of the soul's need for something that would express God's word and then follows this by a discussion of the fact that the Bible is the answer to that need. Next he elaborates upon the nature of the Word that is to be found there and closes without any formal colloquy or application of all this to the will. Instead, the meditation becomes almost continuous colloquy, modulating throughout between calling to mind the sacred truths, looking at them in detail, and subjecting the will to an acceptance of them. In fact, after the seventh there is no longer a place in the meditations for distinct sections; the formal divisions are lost in favor of a meditational form that alternates continuously between praise, petition, and rejoicing, ending sometimes in a separate prayer, but at other times simply coming abruptly to a stop. In the eighth, for example, "Thansgivings for God's Attributes," the ending is in the same long poetic line as the whole of the Thanksgiving itself, and without engaging in self-abasement Traherne merely asks that the principles of the meditation be applied to the will:

Since men upon the earth live in darkness; and are infinitely beneath thy glorious ways,

Let me never be subject to their vain opinions, but ever mindful of thee my God.

To walk in thy ways is to contemplate their Glory, to imitate their Goodness, to be sensible of their Excellency. (285–90)

And in the ninth, "A Thanksgiving and Prayer for the NATION," although he returns to a more obvious colloquy, it is not set out by itself but appears suddenly and briefly at the end in the same kind of line as the rest of the meditation:

O my Lord, where my voice faileth, let love be great, Plead effectually, be accepted graciously. Replenish my Soul, more than I am able to ask or conceive. *Amen, Amen.* (405–07)

Finally, it is the eighth Thanksgiving that seems to be the last of the group which makes up the *Thanksgivings* as a unified meditational sequence. Aside from the shift in subject matter and the tone of the ninth, there is nothing except some of Traherne's favorite ideological motifs to link the ninth Thanksgiving with any that have gone before. The lamentations for the sins and sufferings of nation and people in the first part of this last Thanksgiving are a new departure from the thematic movement from body and earth to soul and heaven in the first eight meditations. In addition, there is at the beginning of the eighth, as at the beginning of the first four, a brief thematic recapitulation of the preceding Thanksgivings. After opening the eighth Thanksgiving with Isaiah 42: 10–12 ("Sing unto the Lord a new Song, and his praise from the ends of the Earth . . ."), Traherne writes a few short lines of free verse, naming the places "In all . . . of his Dominion" where God manifests Himself "To the Understanding." The places become a list of the subjects of the preceding Thanksgivings in their sequential order: "In the Fabrick of my Body, Nature of my Soul, Glory of the/World,/ Blessedness of his Laws, soveraign Providence, Miracles/and Wonders" (20–22). This recapitulation is a clear indication that Traherne was writing the eighth Thanksgiving as part of an ordered series intended to make up a sequential unit into which by subject and general tone the ninth Thanksgiving does not seem to fit.[10]

## Repetitive Style in Embryo

The ninth Thanksgiving may not be in content and tone an integral part of the sequence made up by the first eight, but in style it is a more mature and sophisticated version of what Traherne was working toward throughout the whole *Thanksgivings* sequence, and this style, coming as a kind of culminaton of his experimentation with bracketing and various cataloguing (or paralleling) devices, provides considerable insight into how and why Traherne developed some of the most important features of his language. That insight contains no positive chronology of the development, for he was probably writing his most mature prose (in the *Centuries*) at about the same time he was working on the *Thanksgivings,* but it does give us a picture of the purposes Traherne had in using catalogues and parallel structures, and it provides a view of the way in which he shaped these devices to suit his purposes and made them an integral part of all his work.

Recently Carl M. Selkin has pointed out that Traherne's catalogues are linguistic techniques which "reflect . . . the eternal and infinite One that underlies the apparent multiplicity of phenomena."[11] He says further that the Thanksgivings are especially significant for seeing typographically how these catalogues convey their "meaning" because the bracketed construction shows most clearly the effect of "stacking" items in vertical clusters instead of in a horizontal or serial fashion. The same impression of simultaneity may be created by a variety of similar arrangements of words and phrases without the actual appearance of brackets, but Selkin describes with perceptiveness the relationship of these bracketing devices and catalogues to Traherne's vision of all things existing in the "eternal now" of the Intelligible World. He also correctly associates this vision with Cusa's describing God's reading of an entire page of a book instantaneously. Selkin says of Traherne's catalogues,

Besides their ability to forge identities and force the reader to seek for the underlying unity in their elements, catalogues in Traherne's poetry strive to represent the "NOW" moment of God's eternity (p. 233, 1.145). They are spatial metaphors for simultaneity, a supratemporal phenomenon.[12]

Such a claim as Selkin makes here for the relation of catalogues to the perception of the eternal now is valid, and it is one more indication of the extent to which Traherne's pursuit of the ultimate mystical vision influenced every phase of his language. The catalogue is one of those levels closer to the surface than the patterns of repetition, paradox, and abstraction that work in and around and through the catalogue, but Traherne's language reflects his ultimate purposes on all its levels, and these purposes are seen in all the syntactic and prosodic features his language displays. Thus, it must be remembered that the cataloguing device does not work alone or in only one way, and we understand it best if we view it in a larger context. The *Thanksgivings* offers an excellent position from which to gain such a view.

That Traherne's immediate source for the catalogue was the short-hand, bracketing device in Lancelot Andrewes's *Private Devotions* is almost a certainty. Andrewes's work was not the only example of this placement of words or phrases (functioning as the same syntactical unit) into a vertical column enclosed by brackets, but when his work was translated and published about mid-century it was to his example that subsequent devotional writers looked, and Traherne was one of their number. In Andrewes, however, the practice of bracketing words and other syntactic units seems to have been motivated primarily by economy, to save the time and effort of writing down more than once those parts of the prayers that were to be repeated, simply by making one sample of the phrase stand for all its repetitions while a vertically arranged list contained those non-repeated words or phrases which are to be read as parts of that sample.

In the *Private Devotions* the practice often reflects an efficient, fastidious habit of mind:

from the Spirit to receive the breath
        of the grace that bringeth salvation:

in the Church ⎫          ⎧ calling,
     holy   ⎬ to partake of ⎨ sanctification,
  catholic ⎭         ⎩ distribution[13]

In the *Private Devotions* the major impression is one of efficiency, economy, and dutifulness in remembering all those things for which one should thank his creator. Andrewes's lists are thus reminders to the conscientious soul rather than reflections of the fullness of God and the world. Partly because of the context of exuberant praise in which his lists are set and partly because of the more abstract quality of the lists themselves, Traherne's use of the technique creates, on the contrary, the impression of a limitless and unrestrained pouring forth:


        O blessed be thy glorious Name!
    That thou hast made it,
            A Treasury of Wonders,
            Fit for its several Ages;
                For Dissections,
                For Sculptures in Brass,
                For Draughts in Anatomy,
            For the Contemplation of the Sages.
            Whose inward parts,
                Enshrined in thy Libraries,
        ⎧ The Amazement of the Learned,
        ⎪ The Admiration of Kings and Queens,
Are ⎨ The Joy of Angels;
        ⎪ The Organs of my Soul,
        ⎩ The Wonder of Cherubims.

                        ("Thanksgivings for the Body," 59–73)


In this there is no sense that the meditating soul needs to be reminded of God's bounty. Instead, it is overflowing with a consciousness of divine fullness, as though it were reflecting directly, as a mirror does, the plenitude of God. The body is a "Treasury of Wonders,"and since God has made it an inexhaustible treasury, the wonders it contains need not be displayed in any particular order. In fact, the inexhaustible nature of this treasury is conveyed in large part by the associational manner in which these wonders are described. Instead of a carefully controlled sequence there is a spontaneous bursting forth of item after item as associations of various kinds call each forth in a series that has no logical end. In this way Traherne suggests that behind every wonder in the list there is an infinite number of other wonders that might have been

mentioned had there been space and time, and the reader becomes
conscious of a profusion of riches flowing from God.

This consciousness of the infinite riches of God streaming down to
man in the Creation is one of the most fundamental effects of Traherne's
works, and it is the first, most obvious impression made by the
bracketing and paralleling of structures in the *Thanksgivings*. But
Traherne was not quite aware of the full potential of such structures at
the beginning of the *Thanksgivings*, for in the first Thanksgiving the
bracketing and the lists frequently have a stilted, perfunctory quality
and are lacking in rhythmic or syntactical interest:

Even for our earthly bodies, hast thou created all things.
                    ⎧ Visible.
All things ⎨ Material.
                    ⎩ Sensible
                      Animals,
                      Vegetables,
                      Minerals,
                  Bodies celestial,
                  Bodies terrestrial,
                  The four Elements,
                  Volatile Spirits,
Trees, Herbs, and Flowers,
    The Influences of Heaven,
Clouds, Vapors, Wind,
    Dew, Rain, Hail, and Snow
Light and Darkness, Night and Day,
    The Seasons of the Year.

                                    ("Thanksgivings for the Body," 242–58)

But once he has adopted the basic pattern, Traherne begins in the
second Thanksgiving to explore the stylistic possibilities of this
bracketing-cataloguing technique in a variety of ways. He develops its
potential variations, refines its use, and makes it more flexible.

He is careful, first of all, to shorten individual catalogues, breaking
into them with a structural variation or concluding with a line of
contrasting rhythm or length. But, in addition to shortening the
catalogue and varying its rhythmic pace, Traherne keeps shifting the

part of speech and/or particular word upon which the repetition turns so that it moves like an eddying stream to a new set of variations. The momentum of the second Thanksgiving, unlike the first, seldom flags but continues in wave after wave of heightened religious feeling to the end. In the second section of analysis, for example, Traherne uses the word *power* upon which to base his primary repetitions. The power of the soul to enjoy all things is the theme of the whole section and *power* appears eight times in the next forty-three lines. But while this repetition is going on, there is a continuous display of other, more subtle variations in line lengths, rhythm, and parallel words and phrases which shift their emphases from one part of speech to another:

I have received a Power infinitely greater
　　Than that both of Creating and Enjoying Worlds;

Infinitely more $\begin{cases} \text{Blessed,} \\ \text{Profitable,} \\ \text{Divine,} \\ \text{Glorious.} \end{cases}$

O Lord, I am contented with my Being.
　I rejoyce in thine infinite Bounty,
　　　And praise thy Goodness.
　I see plainly that thy love is infinite.
And having made me such a Creature,
　I will put my Trust in Thee.
Could I have chosen what power soever I pleased
　I would have chosen this;

A Power to $\begin{cases} \text{Please thee.} \\ \text{Enjoy thee.} \end{cases}$

In all the Varieties of $\begin{cases} \text{Works and} \\ \text{Creatures.} \end{cases}$

Compared unto these
　　A Power
　To Divide the Sea,
　Turn Mountains into Gold,
　Command the Sun,
　Trample upon Divels,
　Raise up the Dead,
With whatsoever all the fancy of man can imagine or desire,

$$\text{Is} \begin{cases} \text{Very feebleness} \\ \text{Unprofitable Vanity,} \\ \text{Foolish Childishness.} \end{cases}$$

("Thanksgivings for the Soul," 325–54)

The rhetorical variety in this passage is remarkable. The bracketed portions are well integrated into the sense of the whole line, and the parallel structures are placed in a varied series of rising rhythmic pulses that often end in a contrastingly longer line like waves breaking upon the shore. Thus does Traherne give order, flexibility, and emotional intensity to a mode of expression that seems to have had its foundations in the simple purpose of reminding one's soul of how it should pray and what it should pray for.

The linguistic analogy to the plenitude of God and the simultaneous existence of all things in Him is the reiteration of the incomparably vast wonders of the world, the activity of listing or naming them to the soul. There is little or no need for a linear syntax that places items in a specific order linking them clearly together and delineating their temporal, objective characteristics. Traherne thus imitates linguistically the simultaneous vision of all things by piling up or stacking individual words in clusters without clear reference to a subject–verb–object pattern, either leaving the pattern understood or submerging it beneath wave after wave of such clusters or series of parallel words and phrases.

Traherne adopts the bracketing device of Andrewes at the beginning of the *Thanksgivings* and turns it to his own imitative uses immediately, but, as he progresses, he seeks to overcome its limitations and to give it variety by varying the line lengths and shifting the emphasis from one part of speech to another. He soon masters the potentialities of this bracketing technique, however. Then he incorporates the repetitive material more subtly into a conventional and frequently longer line. The sense of the simultaneity and richness of all things existing in the Mind of God is retained but made more intricate and flexible by the increased availability of syntactic structures in any line or set of lines. Traherne can now include one structural pattern within another like a nest of Chinese boxes so that the sentences flow in a continuous line of meaning while a series of paralleling and contrasting designs move in and around it. Thus, as he does later in the *Ethicks,* he can more easily set one syntactic structure against another, beginning one and delaying its resolution while he starts others in motion, prolonging or resolving them whenever or however he chooses.

One of the most mature and complex examples of this intricate nesting, contrasting, and paralleling of structures we have already examined in *Christian Ethicks,* with its long paragraph built largely upon the repetition of the word *more* in a series of similar but varying phrases. In the sixth Thanksgiving, "Thanksgivings for the Beauty of his Providence," there is a good example of how inflexible and limited the bracketing form is in comparison to the structures in the *Ethicks,* for it is also built upon the repetition of the word *more*:

> Let all the Greatness whereby thou advancest thy Servant,
> Make me not more proud, but more humble:

More
> Obedient to the King,
> Diligent in my Calling,
> Subservient to my Spiritual Fathers, Pastors and Teachers;
> Meek to mine Inferiours,
> Humble to all;
> Compassionate on the ignorant;
> Sensible of my Sins;
> Lowly to the poor,
> Charitable to the needy;
> Loving to mine Enemies;
> Tender to the erroneous,
> > Thirsting their return;
> Industrious in serving thee,
> > In calling them,
> > In saving all. (537–53)

In earlier Thanksgivings Traherne had set brackets within brackets without successfully decreasing their stiffness, and in this passage he uses a similar technique by moving at the end from the dominant adjectival phrase pattern to a series of subordinate prepositional phrases that are similar in construction but yet different enough to provide a sense of variety. Even so, it is obvious that in this bracketed passage the possibilities for variety are limited to relatively simple branching tree

constructions, and Traherne's use of alliteration, assonance, and consonance cannot overcome the inherent limitations of the bracketing
device.

In the eighth Thanksgiving, "Thanksgivings for God's Attributes,"
Traherne, having apparently explored the possibilities of the bracketing
device, turns to the conventional prose line as his main form of
expression, but he does not abandon the reiterative manner which the
bracketing device exhibited. Rather, in the eighth Thanksgiving he
writes a more flexible line and increases the appearance of absolute or
nearly absolute constructions. These devices then become the chief
rhetorical staple of his discussions of the eternity and infinity of God in
this most abstract and metaphysical of all the Thanksgivings:

> The Zenith and Nadir, and the Poles of Power in all their Altitudes.
> That infinite Wisdom, Goodness, Power are wholly mine, in all their
> activities, atchievements, Glories.
> Made so by the infinite workings of infinite Wisdom, Goodness and
> Power.
> In every Soul supreme in thy Kingdom, Crowning mine.
> O my God who could have made every Soul among innumerable millions,
> The end of all things!
> Every one King of all thy Kingdom! (45–54)

These same patterns are used again in the last, or ninth, Thanksgiving,
this time in a rich and balanced combination where the earlier devices of
short repeated phrase and brackets are rare but not abandoned
altogether:

> They are commanded all to love me as themselves, though they refuse to
> do it, give me Grace to love them more than my self.
> As *Moses* did the *Israelites,* David his *Jews; Jesus* Sinners:
> Give me wide and publick Affections;
> So strong to each as if I loved him alone.
> Make me a Blessing to all the Kingdom,
>     A peculiar Treasure (after thy similitude) to every Soul.
> Especially to those whom thou hast given me by love, make me a shining
> light, a Golden Candlestick,
>     A Temple of thy presence in the midst of them;

Giving me power from day to day
       To { Praise thy wonders,
              Glorify thy name,
To magnify the excellencies of thy Loving-kindness in all their ears, and to
publish thy righteousness in the great Congregation. (384–99)

Such language conveys not only the effect of infinite riches pouring
from God but also of a simultaneity of these riches, each distinct and
significant in its own integrity, existing eternally in the Intelligible
World. The ninth Thanksgiving is a kind of culmination of Traherne's
efforts to develop a language that would express the awareness of all
things as living and dynamic yet permanent and immediately present
to the soul. Inspired by the free verse of the Psalms as well as their
quality, their content of praise and thanksgiving, and starting with the
bracketing device of Bishop Andrewes's *Private Devotions* as a means of
conveying his own strongly felt sense of the simultaneity, richness, and
abundance of all things in God, Traherne developed a paralleling,
incantatory style. This style, while simple and plain in eschewing wit,
metaphor, and recondite diction, was also supple, intricate, and complex in its utilization of all the devices of repetition. In *Christian Ethicks*
we see this style in some of its maturest forms put to the use of
theological and moral exposition, and in the *Thanksgivings* we see it in
some of its developing stages.

## Chapter Five

# Roman Forgeries

## Background and Purpose

If Traherne wrote the ninth Thanksgiving as a response to King Charles's unpopular Declaration of Indulgence (March 15, 1672) and the equally distasteful Third Dutch War that followed immediately after, he probably had finished it before Sir Orlando Bridgeman was dismissed as Keeper of the Great Seal in November of that same year. Traherne stayed with the Bridgemans when they retired to their estate at Teddington, and it must have been shortly after the family's removal from London that Traherne journeyed back to Oxford to do research at the Bodleian Library in the preparation of *Roman Forgeries*. He must also have traveled the additional miles from Oxford to Credenhill, perhaps before starting his work at the Bodleian, because his signature appears in the Credenhill Parish Register for 1672. This was also the last time he signed the register and the first appearance of his signature since 1668, the year before he went to London as Bridgeman's chaplain.

Although Margoliouth believed that *Forgeries* was written as "the seventeenth-century equivalent of the modern B. D. Thesis,"[1] Carol Marks has clearly shown that the whole of the work must have been written (or thoroughly rewritten) after the publication in 1671–72 of the *Sacrosancta Concilia ad an 1664* by Philippe Labbè and Gabriel Cossart.[2] Traherne makes extensive use of Labbè and Cossart throughout the *Forgeries*. Thus, because his acquaintance with the collection must have begun early in his studies, the most likely assumption is that he did not start these studies until after the Declaration of Indulgence, the Third Dutch War, and the pro-Catholic policies of Charles had forced the Bridgeman household into retirement and raised a new wave of anti-Catholic sentiment in the country. It would seem, then, that the whole of *Roman Forgeries,* from conception to finished work, was more than likely composed sometime between December 1672 and September 25, 1673, when it was entered in the Stationer's Register. Traherne was still writing the front matter at about the same time the book was entered, for on the last page of "A Premonition" he mentions and quotes from a sermon by Stillingfleet, "The Reformation Justified" on the text of Acts 24:14 (Traherne says 24:17) which was delivered on September 21, 1673.[3]

Although the book does not bear Traherne's name on the title page, the absence of his name was probably not motivated by any fear of reprisal, for his identity would have been obvious enough from the dedication to Orlando Bridgeman to whom Traherne says he "Devoteth his best Services and Dedicateth the Use and Benefit of his Ensuing Labors." There may even be a certain pointedness, as well, in Bridgeman's being called, in a slight anachronism, "One of His Majesties Most Honourable Privy Council," seeming to suggest that Bridgeman's removal from office could not alter his right to advise King Charles. To advise the King was, in fact, one of Traherne's strong motivations behind his book; he wanted to make the King see better where his disastrous policies of war and his flirtation with Roman Catholicism were likely to lead. If the King were to become Catholic he would then be bound to obey the Pope without question and would thereby be placing his own authority at the Pope's feet. Because the Pope is to be worshipped by Catholics as though he were God Himself, such blind obedience could result in all manner of abomination such as "Poysning Emperours, Murdering Kings, attempting on Queens, their Massacre at *Paris,* the Gunpowder-Treason, & c." (*RF,* 316).[4]

The false records and forgeries that Traherne is exposing are the fundamental basis upon which this idolatry of the Pope is supported and thus the direct cause for the Pope's encouragement of such sins—"The *Instruments* of which Acts are by such Records rather favoured than discouraged; and some of them [the instruments of the acts] Canonized, rather than punished in the See of *Rome"* (*RF,* 316). Traherne had indeed expressed his purpose a few pages earlier in discussing the particular false document that openly encouraged such terrible acts:

That Princes may a little more clearly see into the Mystery of these counter-feit *Decretals,* it is meet, in the close of all, to expose to the view of the World one *Passage,* out of many other, which we have passed over in silence. The Design of it touches Kings and Emperours to the *Quick,* though (for greater security to the Chair) it be covertly expressed. (*RF,* 313)

He had made the same point in both direct and oblique ways at several other places in the work (p. 115 especially). He had also prayed in "A Thanksgiving and Prayer for the NATION" to "Rule the heart of thy chosen Servant, our Royal Sovereign, / incline his Will to walk in thy way, and make him thankful for / evermore. / That in his prosperity we may walk in peace" (123–26), a statement that could have been written at about the same time as he was working on the *Forgeries.*

A further reason for believing that *Roman Forgeries* is directed toward instructing the King is that the issue of the Pope's supremacy over all other rulers is itself at the heart of the book's argument. It is unpardon-able that the Roman Church should be guilty of idolatry in its worship of the Pope and that it should be guilty of blasphemy as well as simony in its forgery of documents which support the Pope's supreme and infallible rule, but what is in some ways even worse is that the Pope's supremacy and infallibility destroy the very foundation of all sane social organization as well as all trust in man's rational faculty and his ability to distinguish wrong from right or truth from lies. If the documents the Roman Church alleges in support of Papal supremacy are genuine, then whatever the Pope declares must be accepted as true simply because he declares it. If he should say that white is black and black is white, it must be believed. As a result, all judgment and all possibility of real knowledge are removed with one stroke of the Pope's supreme, infalli-ble pen, and historical records can be rewritten in whatever way he desires. Traherne's argument is therefore against a kind of tyranny that he visualizes in much the same way that George Orwell perceived it in *1984.* Like *1984*'s Ministry of Truth, which constantly rewrites his-tory, the Pope sanctions the making and unmaking of councilor canons and various decretals in order to support his claims: "So that [as Tra-herne says with considerable irony] Antiquities are daily increasing in the Church of *Rome,* and Records are like Figs, *new* ones come up instead of the *old* ones" (*RF,* 109). The Roman Church is like Big

Brother, subjecting private conscience, public knowledge, justice, the affairs of state, and Parliaments as well as Kings to its all-knowing judgment and rule:

For if all are to obey her, as Jesus Christ did his Eternal Father; if it be granted to the Roman Church, by a singular Priviledge, to open and shut the Kingdom of Heaven to whom she will; if no King, Emperour or Council, hath power to judge the Pope, while he hath power to judge all; Kings, Emperours and Councils are made Subject to him, and nothing can escape the Sublimity of his Cognizance. (*RF,* 109)

## In Defense of Freedom and the Establishment

In spite of the fact that Traherne probably would not have allowed complete freedom of publication nor have favored blanket religious toleration any more than his Anglican colleagues, his attack upon the Roman Church was nonetheless based on essentially democratic and progressive principles. The Renaissance had been the cradle of textual analysis and historical criticism, a discovery of original and a reassessment of old documents. The rise of science and the Reformation were both legacies of this same tendency to look directly at the concrete thing and to trust the judgment of the individual mind over arbitrary authority in disputed questions of truth, especially where that mind had access to the things about which a judgment was to be made. The judgments themselves might have sometimes violated the very principles upon which they had been founded, but the principles of free examination once set in motion had their own momentum. Even though the English Church was not the direct result of a zeal for religious independence and reform, it soon allied itself in spirit with the general Reformation and found it necessary to establish its own rationale for existence within that movement. The great apologetical statements of John Jewel's (1522–1571) *An Apology . . . in Defense of the Church of England* (1562) and of Richard Hooker's (1554–1600) *Laws of Ecclesiastical Polity* (1593, 1597) sought that establishment through an appeal to a carefully balanced reasonableness that argued against the irrationality of any dependence upon church authority, scripture, or historical tradition by themselves. These sources of orthodoxy were to be checked against each other and measured by the faithful yet inquiring mind. Fundamental in this approach from the beginning of apologetics for the English Church was, thus, the essentially democratic assumption that no single person or even traditional source was the whole key to a proper understanding of the Scriptures, which were true without question, although sometimes obscure. Neither the Fathers, the Church as an institution, nor special inspiration could be given total, unquestioning allegiance, but a judicious weighing of them all was necessary in order to provide a kind of consensus for belief that would be acceptable to a reasonable mind.[5]

Such a point of view did not mean, however, that the English Church was to be administered by resort to ballot or that every man had the right to believe whatever his conscience dictated, but it did mean that truth had to be sought within the open recognition that all men are fallible. The possibility of error could be compensated for by various means: by the use of logical reasoning, by the general consensus of the early Fathers, and by the ecumenical councils that represented the Christian Church in its original, and therefore purest, form,[6] but not by any single infallible authority. Thus, in opposition to the Roman Church's insistence upon unquestioning belief in its doctrines, the Church of England asserted the power of Right Reason or the ability of the soul to discern truth from falsehood when it was free to examine them both. In opposition to any statement of any single Pope or Father the English Church would assert the broader rule of general agreement or disagreement among the Fathers. And against the dictates of any particular apostolic church, it insisted upon the canons that had been established by all the original churches at the period in which the churches were working as an harmonious group.

Theorists like Jewel and Hooker developed these principles early in the long history of the controversy between the English and the Roman Church, and these principles remained part of the fundamental assumptions of English controversialists, playing, finally, a genuine part in the development of religious toleration, helping even to strengthen the cause of individual rights and due process. In fact, when such controversialists as William Crashaw (1572–1622) and Thomas James (1573–1629) took up the anti-Roman cause after such earlier men as William Fulk (1538–1589), Thomas Bilson (1546/47–1616), John

Rainolds (1549–1607), Lancelot Andrewes, and William Whitaker (1548–1595) had championed it, the analogy to a court of law seemed a natural and indisputable one to make. If truth is to be discovered, the mind must have access to the real facts in the case, and evidence obviously must not be tampered with. As Crashaw complains in the dedicatory epistle of his *Romanish Forgeries and Falsifications* (1606), justice could hardly be rendered if anyone in a court of law had the right to remove whatever evidence he wished from the proceedings. Reserving that right is, as he says, exactly what the Roman Church wished to do by means of Papal infallibility and the *Index expurgatorius,* issued by Pope Pius IV in 1564. Speaking in friendly words to the "seduced Papists of England" to show them that they have been deceived by the Roman Church, Crashaw writes:

Thus is the truth suppressed, God himselfe dishonored, the Authors wronged, our cause prejudiced, the world abused, and you good soules cousined and deceived with their foule falsifications. In civill matters you would think him an ill man, and to deale by ill meanes, who can prove anything, and make men affirm what he list: what then may be said of the Romish Church, who is able to make men say contrary when they are dead to that they did when they were alive?[7]

Thomas James, the earnest librarian of the newly established Bodleian Library, also utilized the same analogy as a basic tool of argument:

For, if in the *Common Law,* forgery, once plainly proved against a man be sufficient to overthrow his cause, be it otherwise never so good; say, in common reason, how are they likely to speed, which to prove a broken title have suborned so many false witnesses, inserted so many words and sentences, and committed so many grosse forgeries, or perjuries rather?[8]

The assumption made by such arguments is the same basically democratic one in Milton's *Areopagitica,* that if truth and error are both allowed a fair hearing in open debate, truth will ultimately win because men are capable of seeing the truth when they are given all the relevant evidence. This is what the moderate Anglicans (as W. K. Jordan calls them) also believed.[9] However, as long as the nature of religious belief was not merely a matter of individual conscience but also of government policy, it was obviously not possible to tolerate any form of belief that would officially deny men the right to an open examination of contending truths and that would insist upon unquestioning faith in some single authority's infallible judgment. Thus, perhaps paradoxically, the English Church could not tolerate the Roman Catholics as fully recognized and contending advocates of truth because the Catholic position would destroy all possibility of debate and subject all the offices of government to one arbitrary and unchallengeable rule. The Anglican's and Traherne's outrage at Charles's Declaration of Indulgence arose from more than a feeling of hostility toward an opposing religious perspective. It was fear of a tyrannical power that had abandoned the ordinary rules of justice, evidence, and honesty in order to support its absurd claims of divine perfection and the right to demand both spiritual and civil disobedience from all members of the Christian world, Kings and magistrates included. The history of its activities had proven that it was dangerous and willing to do anything, no matter how abominable, to gain its ends. One needed only to remember the excommunication of Elizabeth (1570) which absolved of guilt anyone who might assassinate her, the Gunpowder Plot (1605), the religious index, and the existence of that band of professional prevaricators, saboteurs, and followers of Loyola, the Jesuits, in order to understand the serious threat to the whole country posed by the Roman Church.

When Traherne took up the fight against Rome, then, he did not find it necessary to argue specifically doctrinal issues in any attempt to define the theological position of the Church of England—that had been well managed by the early apologists. For him the theological issue was not the important problem, but the moral and political issue was; that is, whether or not the laws of right reason, historical evidence, and common sense were to be abandoned and the reins of government given away to a tyrannical system. Traherne recognized the importance of making people (especially the King) see and understand that the Pope and the Roman Church could not make a legitimate claim to any exclusive spiritual power to speak the word of truth or to damn and to save at will. The idea that it had such power was, in fact, directly contrary to the process of discovering truth in the first place: the application of sound reasoning to evidence that was open and available to all.

One might, perhaps, think that Traherne's insistence that no single person or Church can possess the truth contradicts his efforts, so fully displayed in his other works, to bring the individual soul to a knowledge of and direct union with God. After all, if no one can claim to know the truth—which in a spiritual sense is God—how can one presume to bring his or anyone's soul into union with Him? Although Traherne never confronted this question directly in that form, all that he says about other matters makes clear what his answer would be. Just as the moderate Anglicans and Cambridge Platonists such as Henry More and Joseph Glanvill were in favor of the spiritually inspired man but condemned the enthusiast, so Traherne makes the same inherent distinction between the infinite spiritual nature of the soul and the presumed particular awareness or inspiration that makes one person unique or places him in a position of godlike power over others. Spirituality (that is, being filled with God) is attainable by all, and its accomplishment makes one able to see into the heart of things, discerning their goodness and beauty, but it makes no one necessarily a prophet nor gives him specific information or arbitrary authority over others. Spiritual knowledge is not knowledge of fact or some particular doctrine, but rather simple, undirected experience or loving awareness that draws us into communion as equals, not as master and slave. After all, the essence of Christ's way was humility and service to others, not pompousness and imperious command.

Traherne's approach to the problem was, of course, not original. The Papal claims had been challenged and the documents shown to be false by Jewel and other early apologists. Essentially, Traherne was following the method of Crashaw and Thomas James, which was to explain and collate the forgeries and other false documents used by the Church of Rome to support its assertion of infallibility. William Crashaw, father of the poet who converted to the Roman Church, was a well-known controversialist against Rome who wrote a number of books attacking Romish arguments and activities. In his *Romish Forgeries,* the work most directly relevant to Traherne's book, Crashaw's purpose is to *"ransom and deliver the learned Writers . . . from being worn away and worme-eaten to the heart by Romish corruptions,"*[10] but he, of course, can make only a modest beginning at so great an undertaking and confines himself to the corruptions Rome has made in the writings of John Ferus (fl. 1530), a preacher of Mentz. It is part of Crashaw's purpose, however, to encourage others to carry on the work, for it is a monumental task requiring constant vigilance and many hands. The Papists are diligently altering texts in accordance with the *Index expurgatorius,* and because they destroy the originals as soon as the changes have been made, there is some urgency about restoring them before they are impossible to find.[11]

Thomas James was equally concerned to restore the genuine texts, particularly of the "Scripture, Councels, and Fathers," as the title of his most important work tells us. From a reading of James and Crashaw it is clear that Traherne was inspired by both authors, not only in undertaking the cause of exposing the Roman corruptions in the first place but also in certain strategies of presentation and tone with which he attacks the Church, the Pope, and the Jesuits who have committed so many forgeries. James is stronger than Crashaw in the language of scorn, writing lines that have echoes in Traherne's work. James speaks, for example, of "their impudent approbation, and asseveration of this their lewdnesse and villany,"[12] which may have led Traherne to write several times of the impudence of the Romish proceedings (*RF*, 55, 129, 160). Like Traherne also is James's insistence upon the Roman Church's actions as a form of heresy, whereas Crashaw refers to them simply as foul and unlawful. James writes,

For, if forging of false Treatises, or corruption of the true, changings of Scripture, or altering of mens words, contrary to their meaning, be certaine notes of heresie: how hereticall then must the Church of Rome bee, wherein this doctrine of corruptions is both openly taught and professed?[13]

Such an accusation is a turning of the tables upon the Papists, whose fundamental charge against the Protestants is their heretical falling away from the one, infallible Church. Traherne goes even further than James and makes the accusation of heresy against the Roman Church a ground base of his attack. In "An Advertisement to the Reader" Traherne opens this attack by calling upon both St. Irenaeus and Vincentius Lirinensis for definitions of heresy, the means of recognizing heretics, and the ways of proceeding against them. Then, in his first chapter, discussing "the Nature, Degrees, and Kinds of Forgery,"

Traherne recounts in order of increasing severity the kinds of crimes of which the Roman Church is guilty. Forgery is, he says, very much like "Adultery, Theft, Perjury, and Murder," and, depending upon the circumstances, can constitute everything from simple theft, cheating, and lying to high treason (*RF,* 1). The Roman Church has committed all these, but because it has dealt with Scripture, holy records, and spiritual office, it has been guilty also of sacrilege, simony, and blasphemy—the last because it has fathered its forgeries upon God, "and [this] being done *maliciously,* it draweth near to the unpardonable sin" (*RF,* 4). In this manner, Traherne extends and strengthens James's assertion that forgery is heresy and concludes that the Roman Church "is guilty of more Forgeries than all the Hereticks in the world beside" (*RF,* 6).

Having set forth this severe indictment, Traherne provides a brief historical survey of the early church in order to place the issue in context. It was the general approach of the Anglicans in their conflict with the Roman Church to return to the earliest or primitive church, to the "origins" of Christian organization as having greatest authority, and from there to trace the development of the Roman Church's heresy. Such was Jewel's position, and it was to be an eminently sensible one for the Anglicans to assume, for it was consistent with their reliance upon historical evidence as well as their denial of any access on the part of the Roman Catholics to a continued, special revelation. Jewel had argued that the earliest councils had greatest authority because, in W. M. Southgate's explanation, "they were more nearly contemporaneous with the age of the apostles, with the great period of divine revelation,"[14] and the same primitivism was even being reflected in at least one anonymous pamphlet of Traherne's time.[15] Therefore, when Traherne, in placing so much importance upon the first four hundred years of the early church, seems to display what Stewart calls a "utopian view of the primitive church,"[16] he is, of course, reflecting the usual Anglican point of view.

Traherne's design, then, is simple. He will not concern himself with specific points of theological doctrine upon which the English differs from the Roman Church. Except for such things as *"Transubstantiation, the Popes Supremacy,* the Doctrine of *Merits, Purgatory,* and the like,"(*RF,* sig., B8v) both churches hold the same set of beliefs. Instead, he will attack the Roman Church as an institution and demonstrate that its actions and its claims for itself are not only criminal but heretical. In order to demonstrate his assertions Traherne will first return to the origins of the church and show how the Romans violated the principles and documents of that original church, and then he will follow Thomas James's suggestion to collate all the collections of church documents published by the Roman Church to show the extent to which they perpetuate the same fundamental lies about the validity of the Roman claims to supremacy and infallibility. As Traherne says, "that the Church of *Rome* is guilty in all these respects [he will] prove . . . by demonstrations derived from the Root and Fountain" (*RF,* 6).

Traherne follows this plan by spending chapters two and three describing the organization of the church as it was around the time of the first ecumenical council at Nicaea in the year 325 (Traherne says 327) wherein were laid down the Nicene Creed (a fundamental article of faith in both churches) and certain canons that concern church discipline. It is Canon 5 especially that Traherne emphasizes, for as he points out, this canon expressly states that a person who has been excommunicated by any one of the ruling bishops of the major Church provinces (represented by Sees at Antioch, Alexandria, Constantinople, and Rome) should not be given a hearing by any other single Bishop but that the person in question should appeal to the whole community of bishops which was to consider his case as a group. It was also stated that the Bishops were to resolve all such issues by holding two councils a year so that, as Traherne quotes the canon, "*all Dissention being taken away, we might offer a most pure Gift unto God*" (*RF,* 27). Traherne points out that such a statement precludes the possibility that the Bishop of Rome was understood to have any special authority over the councils or the hearing of any cases outside his own provincial See.

Traherne claims, then, that the beginnings of the notion that the Bishop of Rome had higher powers than any and all the other Bishops came at the time of the Sixth Council at Carthage (418), to which the Bishop of Rome sent two canons (purporting to be from the Council of Nicaea) assigning to Rome the right to hear all cases and pass judgments unilaterally. Apparently the two canons had been written at Sardica, at a council that carried no authority, but in the Roman records the Sardican canons had been written down without being clearly distinguished from the canons of Nicaea.[17] Traherne tells the story this way:

To this Council [Carthage] *Zozimus* the Roman Patriarch sent three persons, one of which was *Faustinus,* an Italian Bishop, to plead his Cause, with two *Canons* fathered upon the *Nicene* Council; designing thereby to justifie his power of *receiving Appeals* both from *Bishops* and *Priests,* but by the care and wisdom of that *Council* they were detected and confounded, the Fraud being made a Spectacle to the whole world. . . . Upon this the Bishop of *Rome* was condemned, his Arrogance and Usurpation suppressed by *Canons,* and his Pride chastised by *Letters*; the Letters and Canons being yet extant. This was done about the year 420. (*RF,* 12–13)

Obviously this chastisement given by the Sixth Council of Carthage to the Bishop of Rome was ineffectual, for he (and subsequent Popes) apparently never acknowledged any error,[18] and as Traherne goes on to say, a contention developed between the churches over this issue, amid which "the Bishops of *Rome* grew so impudent, as to Excommunicate the *Eastern Churches,* because they would not be obedient to an Authority founded on so base a *Forgery*" (*RF,* 15–16). The conflict continued for several hundred years, the Roman Church issuing or counterfeiting various documents intended to make its position tenable, before the first of the collections of documents purporting to be true Church history appeared:

There came out a *collection of Councils and Decretal Epistles,* in the Name of *Isadore,* Bishop of *Hispalis,* about the year 790. In which Book there are neatly interwoven a great company of forged Evidences, or feigned Records tending all to the advancement of the Popes Chair, in a very various, copious, and Elaborate manner. (*RF,* 29)

This collection was of course accepted by the Roman Church as a true authority, and when the Reformation came about, this pseudo-Isidore became the major source for a series of new collections beginning in 1535. Traherne argues that these new collections are a demonstration of the Church of Rome's conscious intention to strengthen the Pope's newly weakened position:

For upon the Reformation of the Church, so happily wrought, and carried on by the Protestants, these *Armies* of *Collectors* were marshalled together, to help a little, and to uphold the Popes Chair by Forgeries: Which intimates a *Dearth* of *Antiquities,* since they are forced to *fly* to such *shameful* expedients. (*RF,* 40)

It is Traherne's purpose to expose the fraudulent nature of these collections by demonstrating how they simply pass on the same false documents from one to another, sometimes adding new forgeries and dropping others that have been too openly discovered or attempting new arguments to cover their scurrilous deceits. The rest of *Roman Forgeries* is taken up with an examination and collation of the collections in a general chronological order and a demonstration of the lies, forgeries, and other various cheats contained in them. It is a huge task, for, as he points out, there are many volumes to be looked at, and although the issue does not interest us today, Traherne tackles it with an enthusiasm and carefulness that are sure indications of his real concern with those problems of justice and freedom that he felt were being raised by the controversy.

## The Style of Religious Polemic

It is true enough that, as Stewart points out, Traherne's method of argument and his way of demonstrating the speciousness of documents takes on a somewhat monotonous sameness throughout the remainder of the book. Much of the time it is a matter of pointing out that a particular author was dead some years before the date at which he was said to have written the document in dispute. It is also true that Traherne, as we would see it now, seems to pounce too heavily upon what he perceives as a weakness in his absent opponent's argument, but if these are any indication of his "uneas[iness] with the formal restraints of disputation,"[19] that uneasiness does not arise from any unconscious feeling that his arguments do not ultimately matter. They obviously matter greatly. They are arguments about politics essentially, not about spiritual doctrine, but they are vital to Traherne because they are the basis of freedom as he then saw it within the general framework of a King, a Parliament, and an established Church.

When Traherne speaks of the many attempts the Church of Rome has made to deceive the world, then, he engages in strong language, mockery, and irony, not only because they were the expected arts of disputation in such a case but also because he believes fully in the justice and importance of the Anglican position. The Church of Rome was a dangerous enemy, deserving the sharp reproof Traherne gives it throughout the book and with particular force at the end, where he warns the reader,

Take heed of a *Pope* and a *Church,* that hath exceeded all the World in Forgerie. For let the Earth be searched from East to West, from Pole to Pole, Jews, Turks, Barbarians, Hereticks, none of them have soared so high, or so often made the Father of Lies their Patron, in things of so great Nature and Importance. (*RF,* 297)

The Roman Church was deserving also of the frequent ironies Traherne casts on it, ranging from sportive humor to colloquial insult and caustic sneer. Traherne was very good at the short, aphoristic sentence, and his direct colloquial language is a major reason one can still read the *Forgeries* with some occasional enjoyment: "*Anacharsis* concerning Laws proved true; *Laws are like Spiders Webs, they detain Flies, but Hornets break through them*" (*RF,* 128). "The more you stir this business, the more it stinks" (*RF,* 130). "He then Clouds himself, like the *Cuttle,* in his own *Ink,* that he might vomit up the *Hook* in the dark, and scape away" (*RF.* 167). "Surely the feet upon which this Peacock stands, are very Black. The pride of *Rome* is founded like that of the great Whore, on the waters at least, if not in the mire" (*RF,* 214).

Sometimes Traherne takes a cool, lofty tone where he feels that the absurdities are openly manifest. At such moments his wry irony is effective and amusing:

The thing is impossible therefore in itself. For he [the Pope] must First be condemned, before a Council could be called to condemn him; and before he could be condemned, the Council must be called. Which would seem among Protestants a Contradiction. (*RF,* 231)

Or, in a somewhat more acerbic form, his mockery of the Jesuit Nicolinus and his collection (1585) is both telling as well as typical of Traherne's most humorous, breezy manner—a blend of casual sophistication and plain man's amazement:

What say you? In good earnest, methinks, the year 1585 is very late, for the finding of *eight and fifty Canons of the Nicene Council*: That Council was assembled in the year 327. and made its Canons above *one thousand and two hundred years* before *Nicolinus* time: They were written in *Greek,* and these lay dormant in *Arabick,* so many Ages, no man can tell where. But the *blessed* Jesuites, or *one of the same Society,* luckily found them the other day. (*RF,* 125)

The language of *Roman Forgeries* is not that of an unpracticed writer, of course, nor is it the language we might have expected after the development of the repetitive style Traherne worked out in the *Thanksgivings.* But the style of the *Thanksgivings* is that of religious feeling and spiritual inspiration; the style of the *Forgeries* is that of disputation and logical explanation. It is basically simple and clear, without any of the incantation that is suggestive of religious inspiration. As Traherne says at one point, "many things more we might speak, but we study brevity" (*RF,* 214). Still, it is a style that is distinctively Traherne's in its frequently balanced antitheses and subtly contrived consonance and alliteration. The veins and sinews of the two styles are the same, but in the *Forgeries* the style is by comparison spare and clean—a proof that Traherne wrote in his most repetitive, effulgent style in order to hold the world up to the reader as a glass in which he might see the spirit and mind of God, not essentially to appeal to the reader's logic or his rational discernment, as he does in *Roman Forgeries.* There are examples of clarity, terseness, and carefully balanced rhythms in the *Forgeries*:

You must touch it gingerly you see, or it will fall to pieces. *Solecismes* and *Nonsense* are like Rust and Cobwebs, signs of *Antiquity* in the *Roman Church*: Else certainly they would never have dared to present such *Mouldy* Instruments to the Face of the World. But such Councils are fit to support the *Mystery of Iniquity,* which is made a *Mystery,* by making and supporting such Councils. (*RF,* 291)

And these stylistic features are capable of blending with the repetitive, incantatory structures of religious inspiration to form the lucid, plain, yet exuberant style of the *Centuries,* which style, whether earlier, later, or contemporaneous with the *Forgeries,* lies in a kind of middle and "perfect" state between the clear polemic of the *Forgeries* and the more profuse catalogues and repetitions of the *Thanksgivings* and the *Ethicks.*

## *Chapter Six*
# Centuries of Meditations

## The *Centuries* and Meditational Form

*Centuries of Meditations* will probably always be the most popular of Traherne's works. Most of the meditations in it are likely to impress the reader as beautifully constructed devotional paragraphs, clear and exhilarating, even though the specific design of the whole work may be baffling at first because its language is diffuse and full of detail. The individual meditations are impressive, however, and they often convey an impression of being carefully crafted, as though the thought were consciously directed through a circular development back to where it began. Thus, the meditations in the *Centuries* frequently end with a sense of closure:

You never Enjoy the World aright, till the Sea it self floweth in your Veins, till you are Clothed with the Heavens, and Crowned with the Stars: and Perceiv your self to be the Sole Heir of the whole World: and more then so, becaus Men are in it who are evry one Sole Heirs, as well as you. Till you can Sing and Rejoyce and Delight in GOD, as Misers do in Gold, and Kings in Scepters, you never Enjoy the World. (*CM* I.29)

And this rounded structure not only reflects the repetitive, circular pattern of Traherne's rhetoric but because it is so well controlled it also helps to strengthen the generally accepted assumption that the *Centuries* is a relatively late, mature work, written some time between 1668/69 (when Traherne was engaged in active study of Pico and Hermes Trismegistus) and 1671/72.[1] Those later years seem almost too full of composition to hold any more, but the rhetorical character of the *Centuries,* written in a middle style between the more spare and direct *Roman Forgeries* and the incantatory *Thanksgivings* and *Ethicks,* suggests the later date. Whatever its time of compositon, however, the *Centuries* exhibits Traherne's buoyant rhetoric in a high state of development.

That the language of the *Centuries* is beautiful, lucid, and often brilliant in effect is not much contested among critics, but the nature of the work's overall design, its structural plan, has been the subject of some speculation. Louis Martz has made a careful analysis of the *Centuries*, and has suggested that its general plan is a Bonaventuran pattern of meditation moving through three stages of finding the traces of God in (1) the external world, (2) the self, and (3) God's attributes.[2] Gerard Cox has argued that the *Centuries* is based upon certain facets of a platonic or "divine philosophy," involving, by Centuries: I, God; II, the world; III, the self; IV, communion with God; and V, the attributes of God, but he regarded the work as "an interesting failure" because "the details of Traherne's prose devotion virtually overwhelm its Platonic structure,"[3] a conclusion that seems to contradict his own argument that there is a "Platonic structure" in the *Centuries*.

Douglas Jordan has made a more relevant analysis of the structure of the *Centuries* and finds Traherne's remarks about the four estates of man—Innocence, Misery, Grace, and Glory—central to its patterning. Jordan says that "the *Centuries* are about the journey of the soul through these estates, teaching the reader how to expand his thought to include all."[4] At the same time, according to Jordan, the more specific topics of the *Centuries* are the world, the soul, and God:

Within the *Centuries,* the "all" is divided for consideration into three main parts: "GOD, THE WORLD, YOUR SELF. *All Things* in Time and Eternity being the Objects of your Felicity GOD the Giver, and you the Receiver" (*C,* II, 100). In his structuring of the *Centuries,* Traherne treats these parts in an ascending order according to their importance. The world is the primary topic of Century I and of Century II through section 69; the individual soul, the topic of meditation from II, 70 through Century IV; and God is the subject of the Fifth Century.[5]

Although Jordan is alone in seeing the four estates of the soul as the controlling pattern for the whole of the *Centuries,* he repeats for individual sections (with some variations as to placement and approach) the same topics that Martz and Cox assert are the bases of Traherne's organizational scheme. These topics are suggested by Traherne himself, as Jordan points out, and they are also the general features of Augustinian-Bonaventuran meditation, as Martz was first to establish.

Unfortunately, the disagreements about the ordering of these topics and how many meditations in each Century are taken up with each topic are an indication of the irrelevance of these topics as the structural basis of the whole work. Traherne is conscious of the topics and talks about them in various ways throughout the *Centuries,* but he uses them for a structural framework only occasionally, shifting from one to another as his larger purpose and the associations in his mind determine. If one earnestly tries to read the *Centuries* in accordance with any of the patterns suggested concerning the world, the self, and God or the four estates, he will soon find the pattern slipping away from him and being replaced by another, which after a few meditations also fades and is replaced by yet one more. One may be inclined, with Stewart, to see the structures in the light of a rhetoric of erosion, but even though the language tends to do away with the ordinary compartmentalization of time-space categories, this tendency cannot itself be a general principle for organizing topics.

If one reads the meditations in the *Centuries* with as little preconceived bias as he can manage, he may simply conclude that they are not constructed upon any formal meditative pattern at all, either individually or as a group. Neither the Ignatian form which Traherne uses in the *Thanksgivings* nor the Augustinian structure used by Bonaventure is in any way decisive for the structure of separate meditations or for the manner in which they are grouped as Centuries. They are, in themselves, freely patterned, devotional paragraphs of varying lengths, much like those recommended by Joseph Hall (1574–1656) in *The Art of Divine Meditation* (1606). Hall's meditative practice had considerable influence throughout the seventeenth century, and it is possible that Traherne's idea of writing meditations in groups of a hundred came from Hall's own *Centuries of Meditations and Vows: Divine and Moral* (1605–1606), although others had used Hall's form and some— Alexander Ross (1591–1654), for example—had also used Hall's title before Traherne wrote his *Centuries.* [6] As Hall describes this form of meditation, however, it is that practiced by "the divine Psalmest," David, who from a glance at the "glorious frame of the heavens" drew a spontaneous reflection upon "the merciful respect God hath to so poor a creature as man." [7] The psalmistic, extemporal meditation thus proceeds by a free play of the mind over the objects it sees both outside and inside itself, making its observations and drawing its lessons by moving from one association to another. This form of meditation is not built upon a directed attention of the meditating mind, and it follows no preconceived formula:

Of extemporal meditation there may be much use, no rule; forasmuch as our conceits herein vary according to the infinite multitude of objects, and their diverse manner of proffering themselves to the mind as also for the suddenness of this act.[8]

The meditations in Hall's *Centuries* are of this short, extemporal kind. Neither singly nor as a group do they follow the Ignatian structure. They are a series of paragraphs of widely varying length, like Traherne's, running sometimes to a page and at other times to only one or two sentences. They range, without any apparent design in the sequence of ideas, over a variety of topics, making a brief reflection on some point of religion or morals or discussing a more complex idea at some length. Hall's Meditation XII of Century I is a typical example, here given in its entirety:

I see there is no man so happy as to have all things, and no man so miserable as not to have some. Why should I look for a better condition than all others? If I have somewhat, and that of the best things, I will in thankfulness enjoy them, and want the rest with contentment.[9]

Traherne's *Centuries* are never as prosaic as this sample of Hall's, nor are they, as Hall's are, without an overall design, however faint that design may become by the piling up of smaller, sometimes partial structures which blend and flow into each other. Traherne's *Centuries* are rather like nature itself—an analogy Traherne would have liked— which pours out and scatters its forms in apparent chaos but keeps beneath its bewildering excess a "straight and regular line." The straight line followed by the *Centuries* as a whole is not, however, patterned after any traditional meditative design. It is, instead, an instructional order, growing out of the effort to demonstrate the great importance of "enjoyment" to the uninitiated soul and to lead it step by step through deeper levels of realization. As he follows his general design, Traherne illustrates, encourages, persuades, and engages in active meditation as each activity becomes important to the accomplishment of his task.

## An Outline of the *Centuries*

When we look at the *Centuries* as a series of progressively deepening instructions in the proper enjoyment of the world, we will be able to discern its organizational scheme from the right position. Century One is an introduction to the whole subject of enjoyment, the secrets of which are about to be imparted. The Century elaborates the general principles of enjoyment, demonstrating its genuineness and greatness, the way it is to be understood and carried out, and the consequences that will follow from either practicing or refusing enjoyment. The Century ends with a demonstration of Christ as the perfect model of that enjoyment, or love of the world, of which Traherne is speaking.

Century Two is an elaboration of how, more specifically, the proper enjoyment of the world will perfect the soul and an explanation of what services the world does for the soul that appreciates it according to its true worth. Century Three next illustrates the first two Centuries by recounting the progress of Traherne's own soul through his infant apprehension of the divine light, his loss of this apprehension because of the wrong teachings of society, and his finding it again through grasping the true, inward meaning of enjoyment. It ends with a confirmation and illustration of the principles of enjoyment to be found in the Bible, especially in the Psalms. Century Four explains in more detail the principles that underlie the soul's attainment of its purpose through enjoyment and demonstrates the spiritual bases of those principles, how they relate to the practical situations of life, and how they are to be put to use. Century Five begins an abstract explanation of the bases of enjoyment in the attributes of God: infinity, eternity, and omnipresence. The Fifth Century ends, however, after only ten meditations have been completed. Traherne must have felt that he had reached a point at which he was not quite certain how he would continue, but there is no reason to believe that he would not have continued had something else not taken him away from the work—perhaps the necessity to write *Roman Forgeries*.

In order to see more clearly how enjoyment forms the whole structural basis of the *Centuries* it will be helpful at this point to have the work before us in outline.

### Century One: *Introduction to enjoyment and description of its nature*

*Meditations:*                                  *Subject:*

1–17:    General introduction to the whole work, setting forth the greatness, yet nearness and simplicity, of enjoyment.

18–20:    Specific introduction to the First Century, describing what the "world" is and what things in the world are to be enjoyed.

21–24:    Explanation of how the presence of desires proves the rightness of enjoying the world.

25–31:    Description of how those things to be enjoyed are to be perceived by the soul.

32–37:    The negative effects of enjoying improperly or of refusing to enjoy the world.

38–39:    The positive results of proper enjoyment—the communion of all souls in God.

40–52:    The foundation and proof of the significance of enjoyment found in the existence of wants and desires in God as well as man.

53–55:    Wants in both God and man as the bond of love—exemplified in Christ and the Cross.

56–100:    Meditations on Christ and the Cross as the ultimate expression of the true meaning of enjoyment.

### Century Two: *The process of enjoyment and its consequences for the soul*

*Meditations:*                                  *Subject:*

1–22:    How the world is to be approached and what services the world as a whole provides.

23–30:    The enjoyment of man's nature as an image and son of God.

31–38:     The enjoyment of Christ as the son of God.

39–69:     The enjoyment of love as an expression of the Trinity.

70–74:     The union and communion of all souls through enjoyment.

75–91:     Union of the soul with God through enjoying the world as God does.

92–100:    A review and summary of the services the world provides for the soul.

## Century Three: *An illustration of the soul's movement toward the attainment of enjoyment.*

*Meditations:*                              *Subject:*

1–6:       Description of the infant vision.

7–14:      The eclipse of the infant vision by the customs of men.

15–26:     Search for lost felicity in the natural world by the faded light of the first vision.

27–35:     Discovery of the Bible as an assurance of felicity, although its meaning is not at first fully understood.

36–45:     The value of formal education and study in the search for felicity.

46–65:     The meaning of solitude and contemplation in the search for felicity.

66–70:     Sudden fusion of knowledge (gained through search) with the meaning of the Bible, especially the Psalms of David.

71–96:     Commentaries on the Psalms and on David as a model of the love and enjoyment of the world.

97–100:    What it means to become a son of God as a result of the enjoyment of the world and thus to live in communion with Him.

## Century Four: *The principles of enjoyment and their practice.*

*Meditations:*                              *Subject:*

1–9:       Perfection requires both thinking and acting well, exemplified in being a Philosopher, Christian, and Divine.

**Century Five:** *The sources of enjoyment grounded in God.*

## Enjoyment's Whole Design

Having set forth the whole of *Centuries of Meditations* in outline we need to examine at least one Century fairly closely in order to understand how the general theme of enjoyment shapes both the larger design and the smaller details. The opening of the First Century establishes the tone of confidential urgency that will dominate the whole of the *Centuries.* By a balance of stress patterns, figurative language, and parallel phrases, the first meditation creates the sense of an intimate revelation of some great and glorious secret. The quiet tone of a conversation with a close personal friend expresses a sense of mutual sharing in spiritual adventure. It will be an affectionate and leisurely talk, one which will lead toward that illumination of soul one had always sought without realizing it.:

An Empty Book is like an Infants Soul, in which any Thing may be Written. It is Capable of all Things, but containeth Nothing. I hav a Mind to fill this with Profitable Wonders. And since Love made you put it into my Hands I will fill it with those Truths you Love, without Knowing them: and with those Things which, if it be Possible, shall shew my Lov; To you, in Communicating most *Enriching Truths*; to Truth, in Exalting Her Beauties in such a Soul. (*CM* I.1)

The repetition of key words—*things, love, truth, soul*—is managed here with a precision beyond that of the *Ethicks,* which was written in greater haste. The repetitions in this meditation are controlled by the principles of balance and antithesis, one phrase matching the other but with enough irregularity to prevent any wearisome euphuistic swinging of a rhetorical pendulum.

The syntactic paralleling of the first two sentences is simple and clear. The phrases that make up both sentences are similar in the number and character of syllables and in rhythmic patterning, but they are not so close in any of these ways as to be intrusive. The first clause is a line of perfect iambic pentameter which is followed by nine syllables that suggest a trochaic character near the end of the line. The second sentence also begins in a basically iambic pattern that is, however, considerably varied and two syllables short of pentameter, but the sentence is completed by six syllables with exactly the same stress pattern as the last six syllables of the first sentence.

The first seventeen meditations are unified not only by their tone of intimate revelation in which the inward significance of the divine principles of enjoyment are about to be revealed, but also by a frequent reference to and variation upon the idea of the "Great Thing" that is drawing forth the soul. Traherne speaks first, in Augustinian fashion, of being drawn to truths that are loved without being known or understood, these truths being the "Profitable Wonders" which the infant soul is capable of but which, like an empty book, the soul has not yet received. The second meditation develops this secret influence that unknown truths have upon the soul and repeats the word *Wonders* from the first meditation (this time as an active verb), emphasizing the marvelousness of the mystery that the meditation will reveal: "Do not Wonder that I Promise to fill it," says Traherne. Then, toward the end of this meditation, as proof of the validity of enjoyment, he explains that the attraction the soul feels for things it does not understand is the invisible evidence of some "Great Thing" that is drawing the soul toward itself:

As Iron at a Distance is drawn by the Loadstone, there being some Invisible Communications between them: So is there in us a World of Lov to somwhat, tho we know not what in the World that should be. There are Invisible Ways of Conveyance by which some Great Thing doth touch our Souls, and by which we tend to it. Do you not feel yourself Drawn with the Expectation and Desire of som Great Thing? (*CM* I.2)

This "Thing" of which he speaks is not seen by the external sight; it is the mystery of God's inward or spiritual laws "that have been Kept Secret from the foundation of the World. Things Strange yet Common; Incredible, yet Known; Most High, yet Plain; infinitely Profitable, but not Esteemed" (*CM* I.3). The one "Great Thing" is, in fact, the truth that the soul is spiritually the heir of the whole world and was created to enjoy it.[10]

But, as he says in the third meditation, this mystery has been both known and concealed since the "Creation of the World, but hath not so been Explained, as that the interior Beauty should be understood" (*CM* I.3). His purpose is to make this interior beauty so clear that his friend's soul will thereby become the "Possessor of the Whole World," a purpose that involves the additional paradox that the plain and open quality of love is at the same time so deep that it contains the profound truth of the "Great Thing" itself. This paradox becomes the focus of the next meditation which explains more fully how important and meaningful it is to become aware of the divine truths of which he is speaking, ending with another, more direct reference to the greatness of these truths:

And I after his Similitude will lead you into Paths Plain and Familiar. Where all Envy, Rapine, Bloodshed, Complaint, and Malice shall be far removed; and nothing appear but Contentment and Thanksgiving. Yet shall the End be so Glorious, that Angels durst not hope for so Great a One till they had seen it. (*CM* I.4)

The fifth meditation speaks once more of a mystery hidden in God since the Creation, explaining that it consists of more than "the

Contemplation of his Lov in the Work of Redemption," that it is also "A Communion with Him in all His Glory" (*CM* I.5). The sixth meditation continues the general introduction by an explanation of genuine love. It is genuine love to wish to impart to another the greatest knowledge one has, but in the fifth meditation, Traherne asserts that this same love was supremely exemplified by Christ in the ultimate act of self-sacrifice. Christ's sacrifice is God's own expression of the desire to impart to another, to man, the greatest knowledge possible, the principle of "true Lov," and Traherne is illustrating that same principle in giving to the yet uninformed soul the gift of that "Great Thing" which love is. The principle of love that Christ exemplifies is also to be understood as a demonstration of the proper enjoyment of the world, and here we can see Traherne's technique of weaving into his work various strands that are apparently dropped but are picked up again at a later time. This strand, for example, is here taken up for only a moment, but it is integral to Traherne's purpose in the whole First Century, for it is part of his demonstration that the enjoyment of the world is so great a thing that it is even attested to by the most significant and fundamental act of Christianity, Christ's own sacrifice on the Cross. But this theme does not appear again until the last section of the First Century where it is developed through forty-four meditations that drive home the seriousness, doctrinal basis, and truth of these principles of proper enjoyment. To convince the soul of this "Great Thing" is the purpose of the First Century, and its culmination in Christ's sacrifice is first briefly stated in the fifth meditation:

The fellowship of the Mystery that hath been hid in God, since the Creation is not only the Contemplation of his Lov in the Work of Redemption: Tho that is Wonderfull: But the End, for which we are Redeemed: A Communion with Him in all his Glory. for which caus, S Peter saith The God of all Grace, hath called us unto His Eternal Glory by Jesus Christ. His Eternal Glory by the Methods of His Divine Wisdom being made ours: and our Fruition of it, the End for which our Savior suffered. (*CM* I.5)

This reference to the suffering of Christ as the supreme example of love stimulates a further discussion of love and its meaning in the next meditation, wherein he returns to the "Great Thing" motif once more:

True Lov, as it intendeth the Greatest Gifts, intendeth also the Greatest Benefits. It contenteth not it self in Shewing Great Things unless it can make them Greatly Usefull. For Lov greatly Delighteth in seeing its Object continualy seated in the Highest Happiness. Unless therfore I could advance you Higher by the uses of what I give, my Lov could not be satisfied, in Giving you the Whole World. But becaus when you Enjoy it, you are Advanced to the Throne of God, and may see His Lov; I rest well Pleased in Bestowing it. It will make you to see your own Greatness, the Truth of the Scriptures, the Amiableness of Virtu, and the Beauty of Religion. (*CM* I.6)

As we have been made aware, this "Great Thing," the proper enjoyment of the world, is to be achieved by meditation or thinking rightly, which, although now more difficult than it was before the Fall, is still easy:

The Easiness of Thinking we received from God, the Difficulty of thinking Well, proceedeth from our selvs. Yet in Truth, it is far more Easy to think well then Ill, becaus Good Thoughts be sweet and Delightfull: Evil Thoughts are full of Discontent and Trouble. So that an Evil Habit, and Custom hav made it Difficult to think well, not Nature. For by Nature, nothing is so Difficult as to Think amiss. (*CM* I.8)

Traherne continues his general introduction to the whole of the *Centuries* by elaborating further on the meaning and central place of meditation as the process by which we attain the purpose for which we were created:

All Things were made to be yours. And you were made to Prize them according to their value: which is your Office and Duty, the End for which you were Created, and the Means wherby you Enjoy. The End for which you were Created is that by Prizing all that God hath don, you may Enjoy your self and Him in Blessedness. (*CM* I.12)

In his efforts to explain this fundamental significance of enjoyment, Traherne returns again and again to the purpose of loving and prizing the world spiritually: "To conceiv aright and to Enjoy the World, is to Conceiv the Holy Ghost, and to see His Lov; Which is the Mind of the Father" (*CM* I.10). And if one conceives rightly he will also realize that every soul is equally to enjoy the world and equally to be enjoyed as part of the world. As Seneca had said, "God gave me alone to all the World, and all the World to me alone" (*CM* I.15). If one knows himself, God, and the world properly, he necessarily will enjoy them all, and it is on this note that Traherne, with meditations 16 and 17, ends his general introduction to the *Centuries*.

At this point he summarizes and then seems to begin a systematic grouping of meditations based upon the self, God, and the world, but the appearance is deceptive. He begins meditation 16 with a summary statement of the point that the whole previous introduction has been making:

That all the World is yours, your very Senses and the Inclinations of Your Mind declare. The Works of God manifest, his Laws testify and his Word doth Prove it. His Attributes most sweetly make it evident. The Powers of your Soul confirm it. (*CM* I.16)

And he ends the meditation with an apparent basis for organizing the *Centuries*: "if you know your self, or God, or the World, you must of Necessity Enjoy it." But meditation 17 is not in fact a first step in the advancement of these themes. It explains what knowledge of God means, but more significantly for the larger design of the First Century, it serves as a coda, restating the meaning of the "Great Thing" with which the century began. The ultimate knowledge of God which the soul seeks is the enjoyment of the world as God's gift:

To know GOD is Life Eternal. There must therfore some Exceeding Great Thing be always attained in the Knowledge of Him. To Know God is to Know Goodness; It is to see the Beauty of infinit Lov: . . . It is to see the King of Heaven and Earth take infinit Delight in *Giving*. Whatever Knowledge els you hav of God, it is but Superstition. (*CM* I.17)

The next three meditations speak respectively of the world, the self, and (varying the themes slightly) the laws of God, which demonstrate that the soul is "commanded" to love or enjoy all things in proper fashion, but this is still not the beginning of any consistent development of these themes. Instead, it is a specific introduction to the First Century, and it divides into narrower units the larger concept of the world set forth in the general introduction. In keeping with this narrowing of scope, meditations 21 through 24 explain in greater detail how it is that the soul's natural desires demonstrate the meaning of enjoying the world and indicate the manner in which it is to be done, summarizing in the 24th the point of this group of meditations:

Is it not a sweet Thing to hav all Covetousness and Ambition satisfied, Suspicion and infidelity removed, Courage and Joy infused? Yet is all this in the fruition of the World attained. for therby God is seen in all His Wisdom, Power, Goodness, and Glory.(*CM* I.24)

In meditation 25 Traherne begins a series describing more exactly than before the way the soul is to "apprehend" and absorb all the parts of the physical world. As he had said in meditation 23, "the true Way of Reigning over them [God's treasures], is to break the WORLD all into Parts, to examine them asunder." And this he does in meditations 25 through 31 by way of explaining how to enjoy the world aright. The meditations in this section are some of the most effective in the *Centuries*. All but one begin with some variation on the phrase "You never Enjoy the World aright" and continue in a kind of incantation to recount each "Part" of the world that must be esteemed in a spiritual manner by "Know[ing] the Ends for which it was Created and feast [ing] upon all these, as upon a World of Joys" (*CM* I.26):

Till your Spirit filleth the whole World, and the Stars are your Jewels, till you are as Familiar with the Ways of God in all Ages as with your Walk and Table: till you are intimatly Acquainted with that Shady Nothing out of which the World was made:. . . you never Enjoy the World. (*CM* I.30)

With meditation 31 the instruction in what the soul is to do in order to enjoy the world comes to an end, and no systematic discussion of such themes as God, the self, or the world follows here either. Instead, Traherne continues to pursue his purpose of establishing the meaning, principles, and implications of enjoyment of the world thoroughly in the understanding of the reader. Meditations 32 through 37 provide a brief negative perspective and explain the consequences of not enjoying the world properly. That men should turn away from the greatest gifts that can be given and spend their time with little, useless playthings is an unbelievable folly, yet, says Traherne, we see them doing it all around us:

For having refused those which God made, and taken to themselvs Treasures of their own, they invented scarce and Rare, Insufficient, Hard to be Gotten, litle, movable and useless Treasures. Yet as violently Persue them as if they were the most Necessary and Excellent Things in the whole World. And tho they are all Mad, yet having made a Combination they seem Wise; and it is a hard matter to persuade them either to Truth or Reason. There seemeth to be no Way, but theirs: wheras God Knoweth They are as far out of the Way of happiness, as the East is from the West. (*CM* I. 33)

Having shown the consequences of refusing to esteem the world properly, Traherne has reached a major transition in the First Century's overall movement. He began the Century by explaining that the presence of desires in the soul is evidence that it is by nature drawn to and created for enjoyment, but he is careful to explain (meditations 32–37) that these desires must be controlled and directed toward the right things. He then spends two meditations (38 and 39) reaffirming the greatness of enjoyment and returning to the earlier repeated phrase, "You never Enjoy the World aright." This time, however, he adds another dimension to the idea that desires are evidence that enjoyment is founded in the nature of the soul. In meditation 39 he re-introduces the motif of the communion of all souls with each other as well as with God, but he introduces a new idea as well, for he adds that through this communion one becomes a son of God. This revelation of additional meaning of the "Great Thing" toward which the soul is drawn deepens the significance of Traherne's discussion by making clear the oneness of God's commands with man's happiness, and it also leads directly to the final theme and argument for the greatness of enjoyment in the First Century—that Christ is the ultimate model for true enjoyment of the world, the culmination and pattern of the principles he has been discussing:

Your Enjoyment is never right, till you esteem evry Soul so Great a Treasure as our Savior doth: and that the Laws of God are sweeter then the Hony and Hony Comb becaus they command you to lov them all in such Perfect Maner.

For how are they Gods Treasures? Are they not the Riches of His Lov? Is it not his Goodness that maketh Him Glorious to them? Can the Sun or Stars serv Him any other Way, then by serving them? And how will you be the Son of God, but by having a Great Soul like unto your Fathers. *The Laws of God command you to live in His Image. and to do so, is to live in Heaven.* God commandeth you to lov all like Him, becaus He would hav you to be his Son, all them to be your Riches, you to be Glorious before them, and all the Creatures in serving them to be your Treasures, while you are his Delight, like him in Beauty, and the Darling of his Bosom. (*CM* 1. 39)

It is this condition of being God's son by living "in His Image" that links the final theme of Christ and the Cross with the first and underlying theme of desires that move the soul toward their satisfaction. We could not be satisfied by living in God's image, he explains in the next meditation, were it not that we felt desires in the first place and actually needed those things that satisfy us. That our souls are made in God's image is a demonstration that the same principle of desires and their satisfaction is to be found in God Himself. It is not that God is in any real sense lacking anything, but only that in God there is a creative tension like that between positive and negative poles. Conceptually, the idea resembles the Taoist embodiment of the opposites, Yin and Yang, in one undivided whole, but it is expressed by Traherne as the presence of light and shade without which there would be no picture:

As Pictures are made Curious by Lights and Shades, which without Shades, could not be: so is Felicitie composed of Wants and Supplies, without which mixture there could be no Felicity. Were there no Needs, Wants would be Wanting themselvs; and Supplies Superfluous. Want being the Parent of Celestial Treasure. (*CM* I. 41)

Later, after he has explained how God both wanted and possessed what he wanted, Traherne introduces the tree of life as a symbol of the desire fulfilled, and it is this reference that becomes the means of transition to his meditations on the Cross of Christ:

Infinit Wants Satisfied Produce infinit Joys; And, in the Possession of those Joys are infinit Joys themselvs. *The Desire Satisfied is a Tree of Life.* . . . GOD was never without this Tree of Life. (*CM* I. 43)

Traherne's renewed discussion of wants and desires, beginning with meditation 39, is an integral part of the structure of the First Century. It repeats in expanded, deeper form the idea with which the Century began, that the soul's secret desire for some "Great Thing" demonstrates the principles of enjoyment, and it introduces the final demonstration of these principles: Christ's sacrifice on the Cross, which constitutes the highest and most convincing argument for these principles, the meaning and validity of which the First Century seeks to establish. Meditations 40 through 51 elaborate upon the general nature of wants and desires in both God and man, and meditations 52 through 55 turn to a discussion of the more specific relationship between God and the individual soul bound together by the "Bands and Cements" of mutual wants. In meditation 54 Traherne first introduces into this discussion of wants and desires the symbol of Christ and the Cross and continues it in meditation 55, which is the preparation for the long series of meditations on Christ and the meaning of his life and death with which the First Century ends. These last forty-four meditations are the only ones in the whole of Century One that bear a close resemblance to the tone and structure of traditional meditations, but the pattern of the soul's immediate involvement with a meditative point or with a direct colloquy with God is broken into intermittently by instruction and explanation.

After reflecting in meditation 55 upon the principles involved in the soul's use of meditation, Traherne draws attenton to the Cross itself, thus introducing the subject to follow and encouraging the individual soul to contemplate the Cross in all its meanings and to expand its vision to limitless dimensions:

The Contemplation of Eternity maketh the Soul Immortal. Whose Glory it is, that it can see before and after its Existence into Endless Spaces. Its Sight is its Presence. And therfore is the Presence of the understanding endless, becaus its Sight is so. . . . No Creature but one like unto the Holy Angels can see into all Ages. Sure this Power was not given in vain. but for some Wonderfull Purpose; worthy of itself to Enjoy and fathom. Would Men consider what GOD hath don, they would be Ravished in Spirit with the Glory of His doings. . . . But abov all these our Saviors Cross is the Throne of Delights. That Centre of Eternity, That Tree of Life in the midst of the Paradice of GOD! (CM I.55)

Here is the connection between the Cross and its meaning as a model for the satisfaction of desire that the soul is to gain through proper enjoyment, for in meditation 43 Traherne has asserted that *"The Desire Satisfied is a Tree of Life."* Thus, the Cross is the most profound example of satisfied desire and the deepest expression of the "Great Thing" with which the Century began, the archetype by which we learn what we must know about loving all things properly:

The Cross of Christ is the Jacobs ladder by which we Ascend into the Highest Heavens. There we see Joyfull Patriarchs, Expecting saints, and Prophets Ministering, Apostles Publishing and Doctors Teaching. All Nations con-centering, and Angels Praising. That Cross is a Tree set on fire with invisible flame, that Illuminateth all the World. The Flame is Lov. The Lov in His Bosom who died on it. In the light of which we see how to possess all the Things in Heaven and Earth after His Similitud. For He that Suffered on it, was the Son of GOD as you are: tho He seemed a Mortal Man. He had Acquaintance and Relations as you hav, but He was a Lover of Men and Angels. Was He not the Son of GOD and Heir of the Whole World? To this poor Bleeding Naked Man did all the Corn and Wine and Oyl, and Gold and Silver in the World minister in an Invisible Maner, even as he was exposed Lying and Dying upon the Cross. (*CM* I.60)

Traherne proceeds in much the same fashion to the end of the First Century, sometimes rising to high emotional intensity in a series of direct visualizations of the Crucifixion:

Is this He that was transfigured upon Mount Tabor! Pale, Withered! Extended! Tortured! Soyld with Blood and Sweat and Dust! Dried! Parched! O Sad! O Dismal Spectacle! . . . Thou wast slain for me: and shall I leav thy Body in the feild O Lord? (*CM* I.89)

At other times he instructs the individual soul, discussing the ways it must respond:

But there are a sort of Saints meet to be your Companions, in another maner. But that they lie concealed. You must therfore make your self exceeding Virtuous, that by the very Splendor of your Fame you may find them out. (*CM* I.82)

But, in all these final meditations, Traherne is working through and elaborating the significance of Christ as the culminating expression of perfect enjoyment of the world. In meditation 100 he summarizes this significance and explains the basic ideas of the whole First Century:

Christ Dwelling in our Hearts by Faith is an infinit Mystery. which may thus be understood. An Object Seen, is in the Faculty seeing it, and by that in the Soul of the Seer, after the Best of Maners. . . . Things Dead in Dead Place Effect nothing. But in a Living Soul, that seeth their Excellencies, they Excite a Pleasure answerable to their value, a Wisdom to Embrace them, a Courage not to Forsake them, a Lov of their Donor, Praises and Thanksgivings; and a Greatness and a Joy Equal to their Goodness. And thus all Ages are present in my Soul, and all Kingdoms, and GOD Blessed forever. And thus Jesus Christ is seen in me and dwelleth in me, when I believ upon him. And thus all Saints are in me, and I in them. And thus all Angels and the Eternity and Infinity of GOD are in me for evermore. I being the Living TEMPLE and Comprehensor of them. . . . Let Heaven and Earth Men and Angels, God and his Creatures be always within us. that is in our Sight, in our Sence, in our Lov and Esteem: that in the Light of the Holy Ghost we may see the Glory of His Eternal Kingdom, and Sing the Song of Moses, and the Song of the Lamb saying, Great and Marvellous are thy Works Lord GOD Almighty. (*CM* I.100)

It is clear that *Centuries of Meditations* is a complex and ordered work and that its order is not in the sequence by which specifically meditative ideas or points (such as God, the world, or the self) are taken up. It is, rather, in the organization of its instructional purpose, which permeates the whole work right up through the tenth, or last, meditation of Century Five. In leading the soul to understand what it is to enjoy and the effects its enjoyment will have, for example, the Second Century develops some of Traherne's favorite ideas in their fullest elaboration: the oneness of all souls with each other through each soul's enjoyment of the world, love as an analogy of the Trinity, and the infinite expansion of the soul by imitating God in one's "thought" or intellections of the world.

The Third Century, although it seems at first glance to be a departure from enjoyment, is an expansion and fulfillment of that very subject, for it leads the soul vicariously through the journey it must make in achieving proper enjoyment. The Third Century contains Traherne's most beautiful and best-known writing, a sense of the newness and brightness of the world in the innocence of childhood being expressed in intricately paralleled structures and clear, simple diction. The Century moves also on another level, through the four estates, from Innocence through Misery to Grace and Glory; it is as a whole a rich blending of themes in which personal narrative combines with objective example, philosophical speculation, spiritual communion, instruction, and direct meditation.

The Fourth Century is perhaps the least well integrated with the central theme of enjoyment. The organizing power of its purpose is not strong enough to prevent it from being sometimes a fairly plain recounting of the principles that are involved in integrating the active and the contemplative lives. The Century ends, however, with an explanation of what will be gained by an expansion of the soul in accordance with its infinite capacity. It will be "A Perfect Indwelling of the Soul in GOD, and GOD in the Soul. So that as the fulness of the GODHEAD dwelleth in our Savior, it shall dwell in us" (*CM* IV.100). This expresses the final goal of the kind of enjoyment Traherne wants to teach, and it is where the first secret stirrings of desire for some great but unknown thing ultimately lead. Nothing is left but to bring the soul directly to an understanding of the divine power behind this quest the soul has been drawn into making, and this Traherne does in Century Five.

The Fifth Century, because of its directly metaphysical concerns, is one of the most interesting of all. Traherne is at his best in combining intricate and abstract ideas with an excited sense of wonder in the soul as it discovers their real meaning and implications. The significance of these final meditations is consistent with the whole point of the *Centuries,* that the proper enjoyment of all things in the world is the ultimate end and purpose of existence itself. Even such rarefied things as infinity and eternity are the bases of our joys: "The Infinity of God is our Enjoyment" (*CM* V.2); "Eternitie magnifies our Joys exceedingly" (*CM* V.8); "His Omnipresence is an ample Territory or Field of Joys" (*CM* V.9). And, although few may be willing to follow Traherne into what might strike them as arid regions of speculation, it is in these abstract and pointedly paradoxical meditations of Century Five that Traherne reaches his most characteristic expression of that form of contemplation that grasps the meaning of time without time, motion without motion, and ages without end. If we can ourselves reach this exalted vision of things we will have learned to enjoy the world as it was intended to be enjoyed—in the similitude of God.

Thus by means of the *Centuries* Traherne leads his friend, the reader, the aspiring soul, from the first recognition of restless desires—through the realization that they are immortal longings testifying to the meaning of enjoyment and validating all knowledge and religion—up to the final recognition that they have their ultimate source in the divine Being itself.

### Enjoyment and the Language of Infinity

The principles of enjoyment and how to proceed therein are the primary subject and structural basis of the *Centuries*. Whatever topics we find of a specifically meditational or ideological nature—the four estates, the self, God, the world, love, the Psalms—are present only to illustrate or explain the various facets of enjoyment as Traherne finds them to his purpose. Such topics may from time to time be the bases of individual meditations or groups of meditations, but they are never sustained long enough to function as an organizational device for the *Centuries* in whole or in significant part.

When we become aware of enjoyment as the real subject of the *Centuries* we also understand how close that subject is to *Christian Ethicks*. At the center of the *Ethicks* is that blending of love and knowledge called gratitude. Every virtue tends toward this gratitude and is ultimately defined by it, for if we can come to know all things as they "relateth to God and all Creatures" (*CM* III.55), we will render to God the gratitude He deserves and will respond to all things in accordance with their ultimate purposes. Whatever virtue we seek is found not in some rule of behavior that identifies it as ours but rather in a condition of the soul that determines the correctness of whatever we do, and because virtue is, finally, giving to all things their due esteem, we will necessarily appreciate or enjoy everything in the Creation. Proper enjoyment, the subject of the *Centuries,* is, therefore, one with the gratitude that lies at the center of the *Ethicks,* and we see again the relevance for Traherne of Cusa's assertion that all theology is established in a circle. If in God to be and to act are the same, any attempt to understand God must, finally, become an intricate dialectic moving around and toward a center, for all objects will be seen as acts and all acts as but various descriptions of God's eternal and infinite Being—the lights and shadows of one supra-cosmic picture. We cannot tell the dancer from the dance because the dancer *is* the dance, and that stupendous fact is what we must come to understand and appreciate.

We have already seen how powerfully Traherne's concern with expressing this vision of the ultimate oneness of God and the world influences his language—his parallel, repeated phrases, words, and images. In the *Centuries* that influence works in the same ways as it does in the *Ethicks* and his other writings, but the meditations of the *Centuries* exhibit that influence in its most effective and most nearly perfect form. These meditations are the most satisfying of all Traherne's work because they were written with considerable care upon the subject of deepest concern to him, under the impetus of a direct personal relationship—conditions which were advantageous to his particular talent.

In style, the *Centuries* lies between the sometimes hasty, unpruned, and densely repetitious character of the *Ethicks* (as well as the *Thanksgivings*) and the direct, plainer nature of the *Roman Forgeries*. Traherne was capable of the short, cleanly focused sentence and the balanced phrase; and much of the excited beauty of the *Centuries* results from an unusual combination of the two. This balanced, paralleling, and ritually repeating quality of the *Centuries* is immediately apparent, as well as its simplicity and clarity:

An Empty Book is like an Infants Soul, in which any Thing may be Written. It is Capable of all Things, but containeth Nothing. I hav a Mind to fill this with Profitable Wonders. (*CM* I.1)

That this style is a more complex and subtle manipulation of the bracketing device with which Traherne experimented in the *Thanksgivings* is also clear, especially if the parallel structures are set out in brackets for the sake of comparison, as in these lines, which immediately follow those above:

And since Love made you put it into my Hands

I will fill it with those { Truths you Love, without Knowing them:
                           and
                           Things which, if it be Possible,

shall shew my Lov; to { you,  } in { communicating most *Enriching Truths*
                       { Truth, }     { Exalting Her Beauties in such a Soul.

                                                        (*CM* I.1)


The greater complexity and subtlety of these lines over most of those in
the *Thanksgivings* is in large part the result of the greater length of
paralleled phrases—and thus greater intricacy of construction—that
can be and is achieved in the absence of brackets. Without brackets, it is
possible to make variations in the repeated phrases so that their sym-
metry is constantly deflected in interesting ways. Such variations are
beautifully achieved—here and throughout the *Centuries*—and this
mastery of varied, subtle phrases and rhythms is a culmination of the
work with bracketing devices in which Traherne was engaged while
writing the *Thanksgivings*.

But there is much more to admire in the style of the *Centuries* than
this suppleness of repeated phrase. The art of the *Centuries* is one that
blends the device of long and short phrases or sentences in parallel with
patterns of closely similar sounds and an abstract diction that shines
with brilliant surfaces. The third meditation of Century Three is the
most memorable and the best example of Traherne's special art in the
*Centuries,* and we turn to it again.

What strikes the reader first, perhaps, is the apparent simplicity of it
all, as if the child who sees the vision were himself speaking in the midst
of experiencing it. Yet it is given in the past tense, the vision not
immediately present but vividly recalled:

The Corn was Orient and Immortal Wheat, which never should be reaped,
nor was ever sown. I thought it had stood from everlasting to everlasting.
(*CM* III.3)

Two short, direct sentences announce the theme, that the simple things of common day are, in fact, eternal and that our first apprehension of them recognizes their eternal nature. The diction is itself simple and ordinary, although the word "Orient" suggests a quality beyond the ordinary, expressing connotations of the hue of wheat enhanced by the golden color of dawn—the time of day being suggested both by "Orient" and by the fact that these are the first apprehensions of the "dawning" infant soul. *Wheat* is itself a concrete word, but the combination of *Orient* and *Immortal* move us away from a perception of the details of the wheat to its qualities of richness and immutability; thus, wheat becomes the immediate expression of brilliantly hued permanence and value. But it is not the abstractness of the image alone that creates the effect of seeing into the eternal nature of things. Perhaps even more significant is the doubling, paralleling, and repetition of structures and words which echo the multiple coordination and polysyndeton of biblical language and create a sense of the continuous, never-ending, and ritual nature of existence.

These same devices continue in the following lines but are used and combined with each other in new ways:

The Dust and Stones of the Street were as Precious as GOLD. The Gates were at first the End of the World, The Green Trees when I saw them first through one of the Gates Transported and Ravished me; their Sweetnes and unusual Beauty made my Heart to leap, and almost mad with Extasie, they were such strange and Wonderfull Things[s]: The Men! O what Venerable and Reverend Creatures did the Aged seem! Immortal Cherubims! And yong Men Glittering and Sparkling Angels and Maids strange Seraphick Pieces of Life and Beauty! Boys and Girles Tumbling in the Street, and Playing, were moving Jewels. I knew not that they were Born or should Die. But all things abided Eternaly as they were in their Proper Places. Eternity was Manifest in the Light of the Day, and som thing infinit Behind evry thing appeared: which talked with my Expectation and moved my Desire. The Citie seemed to stand in Eden, or to be Built in Heaven. (*CM* III.3)

Once again the things to which Traherne refers are specific objects, but they are kept unparticularized. We never see their detail, and they are deliberately brought into association either with a glittering surface or an abstraction suggesting an infinite perspective: the dust and stones are like gold, the gates cover the whole of the world, men are sparkling angels, and the children are as brilliantly shining as precious gems. Overall, the associations are like those in the first two lines, dazzling sensations of priceless value and eternality, which Traherne achieves in much the same way as before, but which are here placed in a series of parallel yet asymmetrical clauses that seem to have grown out of the bracketing device of the *Thanksgivings*. In the *Thanksgivings* these structures might have been written uniformly enough to have been bracketed, but here the shifts in repeated and doubled structures from verb to subject and back to verb make it impossible for them to fit into the bracketing device.

These shifts in established pattern as well as the subtle asymmetry of the combined phrases distinguish these lines as highly sophisticated and beautiful examples of the art of reiteration, and this art of reiteration, of which Traherne became a master in the *Centuries,* does not strive to convey the detailed texture of human experience or of individual objects in time and space; instead, it seeks to name or to catalogue things in order to demonstrate their place in eternal and infinite being—to validate their inestimable worth as expressions of God's own nature. Words are placed in multiple coordination, constructions which present them as individual events, "isolated" from each other and thus not subordinated to the temporal, sequential logic of the observing mind, but displayed, rather, as the unchanging manifestations of their paradoxically immutable but dynamic source—the Divine Intellect.

The things named in this way are apprehended in their "thisness" or ipseity, without any suggestion of their beginning or end, without temporal sequence or relationship. They simply exist, and in that existence show forth God's eternal act: "I knew not that they were Born or should Die. But all things abided Eternaly as they were in their Proper Places. Eternity was Manifest in the Light of the Day." The association of things with eternity is exhibited by the tumbling forth of the names of things in a rush, without connectives, and the excited repetitions manifest the sense of oneness with all things that is felt by the self, whose vison is unhampered by any illusion of separateness:

The Streets were mine, the Temple was mine, the People were mine, their Clothes and Gold and Silver was mine, as much as their Sparkling Eys Fair Skins and ruddy faces. The Skies were mine, and so were the Sun and Moon and Stars, and all the World was mine, and I the only Spectator and Enjoyer of it. I knew no Churlish Proprieties, nor Bounds nor Divisions: but all Proprieties and Divisions were mine: all Treasures and the Possessors of them. (*CM* III.3)

This vision is not possessed by the ego or personal self and is thus not a Narcissus-like appropriation of the world, for the ego or personal self exists only insofar as any boundaries are felt to exist. If there are no boundaries, there is no personal self, and it is exactly this absence of a particular or ego-self that Traherne celebrates as the character of his infant soul. But that state of innocence cannot last forever, and he gradually learns to see things divided from one another and owned by separate individuals.

The end of the meditation comes rapidly. The whole story of his apostasy from this vision is told in a few short lines that read like a parable and bring the lesson in enjoyment to a formal close:

So that with much adoe I was corrupted; and made to learn the Dirty Devices of this World. Which now I unlearn, and becom as it were a little Child again, that I may enter into the Kingdom of GOD. (*CM* III.3)

That it is a lesson in enjoyment may not be immediately obvious because it is easy to misconstrue what enjoyment is from Traherne's point of view, but the rhetoric of the *Centuries* is perfectly attuned to its central message. In and through its discursive, naming, and intricately paralleling technique, its poetic rhythms, carefully modulated sounds, brilliant surfaces, and abstract diction, it expresses a vision of the world that sees it as God's infinite, eternal idea. All of the devices of reiteration are here in the *Centuries* but are more tightly woven than in the *Ethicks,* more fully constructed and shaped into a rounded artistic design. At the same time, the underlying psychological movement toward the final vision of love and knowledge which is enjoyment, is achieved here, as in the *Ethicks,* through the repetition that echoes eternity, the absorption of all things to one that expresses the one undivided in things divided, the central mystery of Being. The *Centuries* achieves its intentions with considerable artistry and develops Traherne's unique reiterative style to its highest degree of perfection. As we shall see more fully later, this reiterative, repetitive style is based upon the thought unit rather than the individual sentence as the source of its structure, and its form arises out of balancing or paralleling one thought unit—whether embodied in a word, a phrase, or a complex clause—against another such unit in a cumulative, coordinating pattern that owes much to Hebraic poetry as translated into the King James version of the Bible. Everpresent in Traherne's mind and his work is the poetry of the Psalms, which he closely imitated in the *Thanksgivings* (combining it with his own adaptation of the bracketed word or phrase), and which he imitated and paraphrased again in the Third Century. Because Traherne's reiterative style relies upon the thought unit as the basis of its form, it is (like Hebraic poetry) a style that depends upon a "prose" structure rather than the regular meters of conventional verse. In it, as J. H. Gardiner has said of Hebraic poetry, "the line [the sense line not the metered line] was the unit and the second line balanced the first, completing or supplementing its meaning."[11] In Traherne's prose, as in Walt Whitman's free verse, all of the devices of image, rhythm, and sound that are usually associated with the structures of metered verse are "entirely dependent upon the thought and structure of the separate lines." [12] What this implies with respect to Traherne's poetry we shall see in Chapter 8.

# Chapter Seven

# "Select Meditations"

## An Early Work

That the manuscripts of Traherne's *Centuries* and poems should have been discovered and a writer completely new to the twentieth century suddenly brought to light is in itself a remarkable story, but that story became even more remarkable when James Osborn announced in 1964 the discovery of yet another manuscript of meditations closely resembling those of the *Centuries*. [1] These new meditations are also gathered together in hundreds and bear the title "Select Meditations," which "appears before each of the last three centuries." [2] That they are "centuries" is also indicated in the subtitles, and these facts provide some suggestion of a deliberate relationship between these meditations and those of the *Centuries*. Louis Martz has conjectured that the two works may be parts of a still larger group of meditations that have not survived, [3] but it is also possible that "Select Meditations" is an early version of the *Centuries*. Unfortunately, any close analysis of the "Select Meditations" on the part of scholars at large is still awaiting publication of the work, a project that has been delayed by the death of Professor Osborn but will, hopefully, be completed by Professor Martz in the near future.

About the probable date of composition of "Select Meditations" there has been no controversy. All who have had the opportunity to read the manuscript have agreed with Osborn's original supposition that Traherne wrote it sometime between 1661 and 1665, the most significant evidence being references to the King in Century I.82 and to "The Government of a Church established by Laws" (III.24), which must have been written after the Restoration, as well as a line about the nation continuing in peace (I.86) which was probably not written after the outbreak of the Second Dutch War (March 1665). [4] There is, of course, a possibility that such a statement could have been made after

131

the war was concluded in 1667. Osborn chose 1661 as the *terminus a quo* because he accepted the general assumption that Traherne began his residence at Credenhill the same year he was appointed, but if, as seems probable, he did not start his duties until 1664, he may not have begun "Select Meditations" before that year either.

## The *Centuries* in Draft

That "Select Meditations" is an earlier work than the *Centuries,* at any rate, is virtually certain. In every way, except in basic ideas, the *Centuries* shows signs of greater maturity, and even in ideas "Select Meditations" seems less sure of itself, less willing to speak from personal conviction and experience than the *Centuries.* Although such a judgment arises largely from the cumulative effect of reading the "Select Meditations" and is difficult to substantiate, meditation 92 of the Second Century is a good example of how much more tentative Traherne's statement of his ideas seems in these earlier meditations than in the *Centuries.* The basic concepts are the same in each work, but in "Select Meditations" they are for the most part presented as distantly perceived notions understood on a primarily logical level, not as immediate truths of direct experience. Its voice is that of a lecturer explaining a logical point rather than of a friend seeking to communicate a deeply felt reality:

There is in a man a Double selfe, according as He is in God, or the world. In the world he is confined, and walketh up and Down in Little Roome: but in God He is evry where. Hence it is that his Thoughts can touch any part of Eternitie. And that his soul is more than the Temple of it. An extensiv and Immaterial Being, which is Like an Indivisible Atom without Bulk, All eye and sight, is therefore evry where, becaus its sight is so, which it selfe is, for the very substance of the soul is all sight, (is when it is perfect as it ought to be,) and pure life as God whose whole Eternity being Incomprehensible, its presence evry where immediately toucheth the soul and affecteth it. which is therefore a Temple or Infinit sphere. (SM II.92)

Such a passage helps us to understand more fully some of the less precisely reasoned statements in the *Centuries* concerning the spiritual nature of the soul and its double existence, but its style is perfunctory in comparison to this passage from the *Centuries*:

The Contemplation of Eternity maketh the Soul Immortal. Whose Glory it is, that it can see before and after its Existence into Endless Spaces. Its Sight is its Presence. And therfore is the Presence of the understanding endless, becaus its Sight is so. O what Glorious Creatures should we be, could we be present in Spirit with all Eternity! (*CM* I.55)

Here the thought has been more fully assimilated and proven by experience, not known merely by study.

These two passages are, however, similar enough in phrase to suggest that this meditation from "Select Meditations" could be a first or an early draft of the one just quoted from the *Centuries*. The phrase "All eye and sight, is therefore evry where, becaus its sight is so, which it self is" may have become later "Its Sight is its Presence. And therfore is the Presence of the understanding endless, becaus its Sight is so." Similarities like this as well as closer ones between the two works can frequently be found, but the order in which these similarities appear is different enough to cast doubt on the notion that "Select Meditations" is simply an early draft of the *Centuries*. In the First Century of "Select Meditations," for example, Traherne begins a short series of meditations upon the nature of eternity, wherein he explains the idea that in God all is present; as he explains it, that which from the standpoint of time is a before-and-after is in eternity a simultaneous existence, and in this simultaneity we participate without realizing it:

Eternity is a Sphere into which we Enter, all whose parts are at once Standing round about us. How else could all its parts before, & after, be objects present to the understanding [.] Eternitie in the Dark is an Object upon the Earth. Therefore Seems an Empty Space prepared before us. But is with God an Eternal Day, whose Evening & morning & Noon are present. (SM I.94)

He continues in the next meditation with an analogy to the process of walking in order to illustrate how it is that eternity appears to us to be the successive "moments" of time:

Tis we are Successiv Eternity is not so. Trees in a walk are past by, Tho them
selves Stand Still. . . . The moments Stand, we mov by, & cry the Time
passeth away. (SM I.95)

In the *Centuries* a discussion of like nature does not begin until the Fifth
or final Century, but there it appears more obviously ordered and more
beautifully expressed. The statement in the *Centuries* is, of course,
extensively revised and expanded from the "Select" version (if it is,
indeed, a revision), but there are still similarities of structure between
the two:

Eternity is a Mysterious Absence of Times and Ages: an Endless Length of
Ages always present, and for ever Perfect. For as there is an immovable Space
wherin all finit Spaces are enclosed, and all Motions carried on, and performed: so is there an Immovable Duration, that contains and measures all
moving Durations. . . . All Ages being but successions correspondent to
those Parts of that Eternitie wherin they abide, and filling no more of it, then
Ages can do. (*CM* V.7)

This meditation in the *Centuries* is followed by further elaboration in
which there appears an analogy of exactly the same kind as the example
in "Select Meditations," although the analogy is changed from a walk
to a journey on a ship:

The smallest Thing by the Influence of Eternity, is made infinit and Eternal.
We pass thorow a standing Continent or Region of Ages, that are already
before us, Glorious and perfect while we com to them. Like men in a ship we
pass forward, the shores and Marks seeming to go backward, tho we move,
and they stand still. (*CM* V.8)

Probably the most striking resemblance of "Select Meditations" to
the *Centuries* occurs, perhaps by coincidence, in the Third Century of
both works. In *Centuries of Meditations* the Third Century is unified by
Traherne's use of his own spiritual history as an illustration of what the
soul may expect in its journey toward felicity, and the third meditation
of that century is the famous description of the child's vision of things
from within the city walls. A remarkably similar description appears in
the Third Century of "Select Meditations":

Gods Kingdom, His Subjects & Laws are Divine Things, when I Look upon them in the Light of the Citty wherein I Lived. I remember the time when its Gates were Amiable, its Streets Beautifull, its Inhabitants immortall, its Temple Glorious, its Inward Roomes & chambers Innocent and all Misterious. Soe they appeared to the little Stranger, when I first came into the world. . . . for I saw them all in the Light of Heaven. They were all mine, Temple Streets Skies Houses Gates and People. I had not learned to appropriate any thing other way. The people were my Living joyes and Moveing Jewells Sweet Amazments walking Miracles: And all the place a Grand Hive, & Repository of Delights. . . . And when I place myself new in that Citty, and see Ages all mine! And Divine Laws & Gods wayes in many Kingdoms. And my soul a Temple of that Day! exalted to be the Image of allmighty God among them all. A companion of Kings & of the Holy Angels: me thinks those are very Glorious things. (SM III.29)

Although this is not the whole of the meditation, it is obvious that it is more loosely structured than *Centuries* III.3. It is partly for this reason that it can serve as a representative of what these earlier meditations are like overall, for they are generally less focused than the *Centuries* in thematic content, vocal direction, and purpose. "Select Meditations" does not appear to follow any particular order in its discussion of ideas, for example, but it is difficult to be certain about any ordering principle because the first eighty meditations are lost. One is led to surmise, however, that in the "Select Meditations" Traherne seems not quite certain of his theme or through what organizational principles to present it. He does not appear to begin with simple ideas and move by degrees into fuller, more complex explanations of felicity, as he does in the *Centuries*. Instead, he seems to shift without conscious design from one level of thought to another. Thus, nearly all of the themes of the *Centuries* can be found in "Select Meditations," but they are scattered and evidently given none of the progressive order of a deepening series of instructions in spiritual understanding that is present in the *Centuries*. In the First Century of "Select Meditations," for instance, Traherne mixes lament for the nation and for wasted souls with complex explanations of time, eternity, and the nature of the soul as the infinite sphere, but he seems to provide no thematic or instructional principle that would bring them all into logical relationship.[5] At the same time, Traherne often shifts vocal direction from the reader to God or to himself without any apparent purpose or warning.

Meditation 29 of the Third Century of "Select Meditations" can be taken as a final example typical of the work as a whole. Instead of beginning directly with the childhood vision itself, it opens with a somewhat awkward explanation, placing the vision in a context of a larger understanding. Then it speaks of "Amiable gates," "immortal inhabitants," and "chambers" that are "Innocent and all Misterious," none of which is as appropriate an adjective for directly conveying the sense of things seen in the light of eternity as those in the *Centuries,* where that sense is conveyed by brilliant and appropriate description. An example of repetitive style follows meditation 29 in "Select Meditations," but the choice of words is, again, not made with a very clear sense of either a unified connotative effect or a clear pattern of sound. Thus we have "Streets Skies House Gates and People" or "And all the place a Grand Hive, and Repository of Delights" instead of "the Skies were mine, and so were the Sun and Moon and Stars." Nor does meditation 29 move to a rounded, tightly focused conclusion as does its counterpart in the *Centuries.*

Perhaps when "Select Meditations" is finally published an organizing theme wll become discernable, but the evidence seems to indicate rather that this latest discovery is written without any special thematic center, before Traherne had fully achieved his unique style, and then either rewritten or (at least) partly used later for a new set of meditations (the *Centuries*) after he found a central meaning and design to give them artistic unity. "Select Meditations," at the very least, strengthens our growing recognition of Traherne as a conscious artist and makes it certain that the *Centuries* is not a work inspired simply by a close personal friendship. Although most likely addressed verbally to Susanna Hopton, the multiple voices of the *Centuries* are spoken to every potential reader and to all human souls. But in "Select Meditations" those voices seem uncertain of themselves as well as unsure of the direction toward which they are speaking, and the result is that the work does not have quite the same high level of appeal as the *Centuries,* nor is it possible to find in it much more than tentative examples of the repetitive, paralleling style that is exhibited in its maturity in the *Centuries.*

## Chapter Eight

# The Poems

## The Two Manuscripts

When the poems of the Dobell manuscript, which were arranged and set down by Thomas Traherne himself, were first published (1903) there was no recognition that they made up any kind of sequence or that their philosophic perspective differed in any way from the Burney group of poems arranged by his brother Philip. Early critical opinion of the poetry was, therefore, based upon a reading of either Thomas's or Philip's version of the poems indiscriminately (Gladys Wade even preferring many of Philip's changes in the poems over what Thomas himself had written). Not until the Dobell Folio began to be recognized, in A. L. Clements's words, as a "unified, coherent sequence of poems,"[1] did critics begin to look closely at Traherne's distinct qualities as a poet and try to understand their relationship to his mystical thought.

Thus far there have been (by A. L. Clements) one book-length study of the poems in the Dobell sequence and a shorter book by Alison Sherrington on "mystical symbolism" in the poetry,[2] two valuable and perceptive chapters on the poems of both the Dobell and Burney manuscripts by Stanley Stewart, and a number of articles on individual poems. These studies are only a beginning in dealing with the problems of reading Traherne's poetry, however, and at least one significant critical question remains in the foreground. That is the question of how much and what kind of authority can be attributed to each of the two poetic sequences. Although Clements rightly argues that for knowing what Thomas Traherne intended in any individual poem we can trust only the Dobell Folio, it is not equally clear that the Dobell arrangement of the poems represents Traherne's final or even the best example of his intentions. The problems are too many and too complex to be discussed at length, but they involve the fact that the changes in the arrangement of poems made by Philip in the Burney group do not alter the basic meaning of the Dobell sequence but, instead, extend some aspects of that meaning over a longer series of poems, delaying the resolution of the meaning and moving it through additional thematic material. Also, as we have seen, the additional thematic material gives the new Burney sequence the same narrative character as the Third Century of the *Centuries of Meditations* and the seventh Thanksgiving— the story of the soul's apostasy and the recovery of its original vision through the discovery of the Bible. These themes complicate the meaning of the sequences, but because they are thus also to be found in other works with which Philip did not tamper, we are forced to assume that both sequential arrangements of the poems are equally representative of Thomas's intentions. We cannot know what Thomas would have done with those poems he did not include in the Dobell Folio, but that he might well have arranged them in a way similar to his arrangement of the same themes in the *Centuries* and the *Thanksgivings* is more than probable. For a full understanding of all Traherne's poems in their contexts, then, one must read through both the Dobell and the Burney sequences in their complete texts as they have been arranged; but because so much difficulty exists in obtaining a full view of the sequences, some description of their character must be given before individual poems are discussed.[3]

Philip's changes in the order of the poems are actually few, and he keeps Thomas's order of the first four poems, which make up a group celebrating the infant soul's first vision of the world: "The Salutation," "Wonder," "Eden," and "Innocence."

In the Dobell Folio the four opening poems are followed by "The Preparative," which is not very directly expressive of the experience of eternity "Manifest in the Light of the Day," but it is explanatory of the meaning of that experience. Thus "The Preparative" is a kind of transition to the next series of poems in the Dobell sequence, which seems to concentrate on the loss of the infant's vision and the soul's efforts to regain it. In the Burney sequence, however, Philip inserted two new poems, "An Infant-Ey" and "The Return," immediately before "The Preparative." These poems are thematically the same as "The Preparative" and explain even more explicitly the need of the soul

to regain its early vision. "But Wantonness and Avarice got in/And
spoil'd my Wealth," he says in "An Infant-Ey," and in "The Return,"
he cries:

To Infancy, O Lord, again I com,
    That I my Manhood may improv:
    My early Tutor is the Womb;
      I still my Cradle lov.
    'Tis strange that I should Wisest be,
    When least I could an Error see. (1–6)

The effect of the new poems is thus to lengthen the theme somewhat,
clarify its meaning, and thereby prepare for the questions in "The
Rapture" (retained also in Burney) which seek to know the source of
all the glory to which he was made heir: "To all this Sacred Wealth, /
This Life and Health, / Who raisd? Who mine / Did make the same?"
(17–20).

    In the Dobell sequence these questions from "The Rapture" are
followed by "The Improvement," which begins: "'Tis more to recollect, then make. The one / Is but an Accident without the other." But
immediately after "The Rapture" in the Burney sequence Philip has
inserted a group of sixteen new poems that are thematically close to
the Third Century of *Centuries of Meditations,* beginning in fact with
"News," which as "On News" is meditation 26 of that Century. "On
News" seems to describe what "The Rapture" implies, that the soul is
beginning to search for something outside itself to verify and reestab-
lish its lost vision:

    What Sacred Instinct did inspire
My Soul in Childhood with a Hope so Strong?
    What Secret Force movd my Desire,
To Expect my Joys beyond the Seas, so Yong?
. . . . . . . . . . . . . . . . . . . . . . . . . .
    I Thirsted Absent Bliss,
And thought that sure beyond the Seas,
Or els in som thing near at hand
I knew not yet, (since nought did pleas
    I knew) my Bliss did stand. (29–32, 38–42)

This new group of poems continues in the Burney manuscript to recount the story of the soul's quest and its final discovery of the Bible, which brings the soul to the communion of "Christendom" and a vision of the heavenly city with its celebration of Christmas bells and churches. "Misapprehension," the last of the new group, is an excellent prelude to "The Improvement," at which poem the Burney group rejoins the Dobell. The last stanza of "Misapprehension" speaks of the world as being apprehended and "recreated" in the mind of man—exactly the point of "Tis more to recollect, then make," which is the first line of "The Improvement." Thus Philip's group of new poems seems to sharpen and clarify some of the themes in the Dobell sequence rather than change or distort them.

After this group of new poems in the Burney sequence, Philip retains the next fourteen Dobell poems (including "The Improvement") but adds another five to them—two following "The Improvement," one about nine poems later, and two toward the end of the group of fourteen Dobell poems. He also changes the order of some of the poems, but the most important change he makes is to excise the last fifteen poems of the Dobell group altogether (all those after "The Enquirie") and put in their place another group of sixteen new poems whose major theme is the nature of the soul's "thoughts," or "apprehensions" of the world. These poems begin with the tentative discussion of the mirrored world in "Shadows in the Water" and similar poems, move through an affirmation of the meaning and power of thoughts in such poems as "Dreams" and "The Inference" (I & II), and finally break free of all boundaries and bonds in "Hosanna": "No more shall Walls, no more shall Walls confine / That glorious Soul which in my Flesh doth shine." The Burney sequence ends with two short poems after "Hosanna" that are to an extent a summing up of what has gone before, moving full circle from the infant vision to its reestablishment in maturity:

> My Child-hood is a Sphere
> Wherin ten thousand hev'nly Joys appear:
> > Those *Thoughts* it doth include,
> > And those Affections, which review'd,
> > > Again present to me
> In better sort the *Things* which I did see
> . . . . . . . . . . . . . . . . . . . . . . . . . .

Which makes my Life a Circle of Delights;
A hidden Sphere of obvious Benefits:
An Earnest that the Actions of the Just
Shall still revive, and flourish in the Dust.

("Review II," 1–6; 9–12)

In the fifteen final poems of the Dobell sequence there is also a concentration upon the meaning of thoughts as reflections of God's Creation in the soul, "the fruit of all his Works" ("Thoughts II"), but there is less personal or detailed imagery, more abstract, philosophical statement in this group than in the corresponding Burney group. The final poem ("Goodnesse") in the Dobell group is a noteworthy exception; in its celebration of the communion of souls it breaks forth in the last two stanzas with Traherne's most sensuous imagery, mingling the warmth of "Swelling Grapes" with soft lips and harmonious tongues. Generally, however, the level of particularization is greater in the Burney poems, partly because they tell a more specific and externalized narrative, but this is the major difference between the two sequences. Their philosophic perspectives are the same (except that the sharpness of specific metaphysical and mystical ideas is dulled by Philip's changes), and the general pattern, celebrating the stages of the soul's journey from innocence through apostasy to redemption, is alike in both, ending in Dobell with the redeemed soul in communion with other souls and in the Burney sequence with the soul breaking out of the bondage of temporal limitations. There are further differences brought about by Philip's alterations in the order of the poems, but those alterations do not create a distinctly new statement out of the Burney poems, nothing that can be confidently claimed is Philip's intention alone. Thus, any full reading of the poems must accept them where they are located in both of the sequences without assuming that one ordering of the poems is necessarily superior to the other. The only proviso is that Thomas's versions alone (insofar as they are available) can be accepted as the proper texts for individual poems.

## Traherne as Poet

Both Clements and Stewart have helped us to appreciate Traherne's poetry more fully, and each has attempted to find the key that will unlock the special nature of Traherne's poetic so that we might finally

understand how to approach his poems. To a generation of readers who
have been schooled on the strong lines, startling images, and complex
ironies of the metaphysical poets, however, the abstract, repetitious
language of Traherne seems dull and flabby. Outside of a few felicitous
phrases and a naive charm, Traherne's poetry appears to have little to
offer those who have been taught to look for a close integration between
prosody and image or irony and concrete detail. In an attempt to answer
such a complaint Clements has argued that Traherne's repetitive,
appositive style is directly suited to his attempt to reveal the ultimate
reality of the spirit to us and to "impart to us Self-knowledge and the
. . . Joy consequent upon it." Clements explains that

He may be spoken of as making series of attempts, aiming series of shots at a
target, in the hope that one or more series will for one or another reader hit
the mark. In Traherne's poetry, the means of expression are suited to the . . .
reader's mode of apprehension: direct, immediate, intuitive, open-eyed.[4]

Stewart, on the other hand, views Traherne's style in relation to a
number of motivations, including the concern for expressing powerful
emotion, for which purpose (Stewart points out) Traherne might have
followed Puttenham's recommendation of the "heaping figure" in *The
Art of English Poetry* (1589), but Stewart's most frequently stated
explanation is Traherne's interest in the expansion of the soul's vision of
the universe.[5] Although Stewart does not explore the philosophic
background of this motif of expansion very far into Traherne's thought
and its sources, its influence upon both his poetry and his prose is
unquestionable. At the same time, Clements's analysis of the mystical
doctrines that underlie Traherne's poetic structures and images is just
and valuable, and it places Traherne in the tradition to which he
belongs.

　　Neither explanation by these two critics goes as far toward defining
Traherne's poetic as we would like, however, and to pursue the problem
further it is necessary to return to the influence of Traherne's unitive
vision upon his prose. We have seen the relationship between Traherne's
understanding of the presence of all things in the mind of God and his
repetitive and paralleling prose structures in such works as the
*Thanksgivings,* the *Centuries,* and the *Ethicks,* where he moved from the
Psalms and a bracketing device in imitation of Andrewes's *Private*

*Devotions* to more intricate and sophisticated syntactical forms. In prose he could, of course, shift freely from association to association and from structure to structure, and in his search for a rhetorical form that would express both the simultaneity and richness of things and their "fixed" nature in relation to an infinite, eternal center, Traherne found the flexibilities of prose exactly suited to his needs. In prose he could use the devices of naming, synonymous phrase, rhythm, and sound patterns of every variety in an organically related movement with the thought unit. Thus Traherne, like Walt Whitman, whose verse forms his prose resembles, found a free or "open" style properly suited to his mystical perspective. As Gay Wilson Allen has said of Whitman's free verse, this is

an enumerative style, [a] cataloging of a representative and symbolical succession of images, conveying the sensation of pantheistic unity and endless becoming.[6]

And Traherne's is a style even more fully grounded in the cadence of the Bible than Whitman's, for Traherne consciously worked through and expressly imitated the Psalms on several occasions. As a style it reaches its highest level of literary quality in the *Centuries,* where it is beautifully adapted to Traherne's cosmic vision, but when he took up the more extrinsically controlled forms of conventional verse, his efforts were not so well rewarded. The conventions of stanzaic structure, fixed rhythmic patterning, uniform line length, and regular rhyme scheme forced him into what was apparently an arbitrary controlling of the flowing, biblically oriented parallel structures that more appropriately express his vision.

In order to understand the meaning of these influences on Traherne's poetic, Kenneth Burke's early (1931) and stimulating classification of literary forms is particularly useful. Burke's definition of *repetitive form* is clearly applicable to the Hebraic paralleling structures which Allen has likened to the free verse patterns of Whitman. Repetitive form "is basic to any work of art," but in its simplest conception it is "the consistent maintaining of the same thing in different ways."[7] This restatement can be made through various details, and in the Hebraic or biblical verse it is made primarily by the thought unit, which may be embodied in a phrase or a whole sentence usually joined to a second unit by a coordinating or paralleling structure that repeats in incantatory fashion the basic idea of the first statement, as in Psalm 83: "Keep not thou silence, O God: hold not thy peace, and be not still. O God. For Lo, thine enemies make a tumult: and they that hate thee have lifted up the head." It is this kind of repetitive form to which Traherne was led by the force of his vision, and it is this form that becomes deeply ingrained in his way of thinking and expression.

What Burke describes as *conventional form,* that form "involv[ing] . . . the appeal of form *as form,*"[8] is also meaningful for understanding Traherne's poetry more clearly, for it is the conventional poetic form that conflicted with Traherne's more natural tendency toward repetitive structures. Because Traherne's orientation was so strongly toward the repetitive form of biblical verse, he seems to have found the usual verse forms awkward and difficult to control. Repetitive, biblical verse does not follow a strict metrical design but moves by a variable rhythmic pattern and line length to parallel the thought and the expression of the preceding line. The sound effects and the imagery that are to be found in this repetitive form arise out of, and are integrated with, this freely flowing line, a line which is based neither upon any regular rhythm and rhyme nor upon the number of syllables the line contains.

The models for poetry that Traherne had other than the Bible were those supplied by such men as Donne, Herbert, Denham, Waller, and similar poets, all of whom wrote in conventional, metrical, and rhymed verse forms. Milton's blank verse was not published until 1667, and partly because its use was thought to be "epical" in nature its influence over lesser kinds of poetry was not felt for some time. The models for religious lyric to which Traherne could reasonably look were therefore all of the conventional, rhymed, and metrical kind even though, as Herbert established, there was considerable variation in stanzaic patterns. When Traherne wrote poetry, such models were too strong for him to ignore, but his orientation for the biblically based, repetitive, paralleling style pulled him in another direction. As one reads Traherne's prose, where the expected patterns of the line are not exact or rigid, one feels no sense of strain or awkward reaching after a particular rhyme, rhythmic pattern, or image; but in the poetry the pull of repetitive form frequently forces Traherne away from a close attention to the demands of lyric verse, affecting even his choice of image.

If one looks again at meditation three of the Third Century, for example, and compares its structural patterns with the poem "Wonder," which reads somewhat like a verse rendering of that same meditation, the tension Traherne apparently felt between his natural repetitive orientation and his conventional verse models can be sensed immediately. Here are the most relevant lines of the third meditation arranged to demonstrate their parallel structures:

The Streets were mine,
the Temple was mine,
the People were mine,
their Clothes and Gold and Silver was mine,
    as much as their Sparkling Eys
                Fair Skins and
                ruddy faces.
The Skies were mine,
    and so were the Sun and Moon and Stars,
and all the World was mine,
    and I the only Spectator and Enjoyer of it.        (17–22)

From the structural repetitions and the subtle asymmetry through variations in phrases and sound patterns, it is apparent that the unit of thought determines the basic rhetorical movement; that is, the choice of phrase and word arises primarily out of the force of the idea as it is felt, not out of the influence of conventional lyric form. The frequent repetition of "mine," for example, which does not function here as formal rhyme, and the variation of syllable and sound in the repeated structures are governed by the intrinsic demands of thought and feeling, not by an extrinsic necessity for rhyme or a predictable pattern of syllabic stress. Without such a necessity the lines seem to develop on their own a supple, varied pattern of aliteration, assonance, and rhythm.

The effect of spontaneous movement which the lines convey is thus dependent upon an open, free, or loose relationship among the various patternings of rhythm and sound. There is order, but that order, as in nature itself, is hidden from immediate view by an apparent profusion of items that appear to go to waste—catalogues, repeated phrases that do not carry any progressive motion or logical weight. By the same token, the meditation does not develop through an essentially metaphoric structure. In fact, neither Traherne's prose nor his poetry contains an abundance of metaphor, and Traherne seldom makes an ordered interrelationship of connotations (which metaphor involves) an integral part of any structure. Traherne's vision of the universe requires simply that for "any thing [to be] found . . . an infinit Treasure, its Place must be found in Eternity, and in Gods Esteem" (*CM* III.55); its place in relation to other things on the temporal or existential plane (to which metaphor calls attention) is irrelevant to that vision, although not always in conflict with it.

For Traherne, then, besides the fact that it may "gild the Sence," and thus obscure the real meaning of one's statement, metaphor tends to fix the soul's vision upon temporal relations between things instead of upon the relation of temporal things to eternity. Such fixing of the attention upon temporal relations results from metaphor, regardless of what images are brought together in it or of how the association of these images is achieved. Given Traherne's overwhelming commitment to the vision of all things in eternity, his indifference to metaphor and poetic structures based upon metaphor is not surprising. Those features of verse that contribute to the effectiveness of metaphor are of little interest to him, and when he writes a poem he often finds such things arbitrary hurdles to be leaped on the way to expression rather than instruments by which that expression can be shaped and given power. In stanza 5 of "Wonder" Traherne expresses the same ideas as he does in the Third Meditation of Century Three, but here the pressures of versification seem to weigh upon his pen:

> The Streets were pavd with Golden Stones,
>     The Boys and Girles were mine,
> Oh how did all their Lovly faces shine!
>     The Sons of Men were Holy Ones.
> Joy, Beauty, Welfare did appear to me,
>         And evry Thing which here I found,
>     While like an Angel I did see,
>             Adornd the Ground.
>
>                                 ("Wonder," 33–40)

The stanza form is almost certainly Traherne's own choice, for he followed Herbert in the invention of new ones for nearly every poem, but once having determined upon it he seems to feel its confining character. Instead of the freedom to chant "the Streets were mine, The Temple was mine, the people were mine" he is apparently faced with the necessity to write a line of tetrameter, a line of trimeter, and then one of pentameter within which he must find a rhyme for "mine" because, in conventional verse, two or three "mines" in a row are not allowed. Thus, the ten syllables of the third line seem pushed into place behind the inevitable "shine," and the spontaneous directness in the *Centuries* of "Sparkling Eys fair Skins and ruddy faces"—which here becomes "Oh how did all their Lovly faces shine!"—is lost behind the wall of foot length and rhyme scheme.

A similar falling off of poetic character takes place in the last four lines of the stanza where Traherne inserts a brief catalogue—"Joy, Beauty, Welfare"—that has no apparent principle of order, traps himself into several lines of awkward syntax, and ends with a rather neutral four-syllable line, "Adornd the Ground," that has what seems to be an unintentionally ambiguous connection with the preceding syntax. The difficulty does not appear to spring from any basic inability to write a proper line of verse but rather from Traherne's desire to write in a repetitive, biblical form. He tends almost always to ignore the demands of conventional verse structure and to avoid the integrated metaphoric image, for the images he seeks are those that demonstrate the oneness of all in God. He is indifferent to the rhetorical devices through which the working out of temporal relations is conventionally achieved. The vision he refers to in this stanza is "like an Angel," and it sees the streets as though they were paved with gold, but this is a commonplace description rather than a metaphor, and the statements in the stanza are related not metaphorically, but adjectivally and statically by holding a mirror up to things and reflecting their eternal gloriousness without relating one to another. When Traherne tries to confine his repetitive structures to conventional verse, its inappropriateness for them and for the vision they are designed to express often appears as awkward, flat, and "unpoetic" lines. In "The Improvement," for example, the perception of everything in one vast, divine

unity focused in the soul is expressed characteristically:

5

His Wisdom, Goodness, Power, as they unite
All things in one, that they may be the *Treasures*
Of one *Enjoy'r,* shine in the utmost Height
They can attain; and are most Glorious *Pleasures,*
    When all the Univers conjoynd in one,
    Exalts a Creature, as if that alone.


6

To bring the Moisture of far distant Seas
Into a *point,* to make them present here,
In *virtu,* not in *Bulk*; one man to pleas
With all the *Powers* of the Highest Sphere,
    From East, from West, from North and South, to bring
    The pleasing *Influence* of evry thing;


7

Is far more *Great* then to Creat them there
Where now they stand; His *Wisdom* more doth shine
In that, his *Might* and *Goodness* more appear,
In recollecting; He is more *Divine*
    In making evry Thing a Gift to one
    Then in the Parts of all his Spacious *Throne.*

("The Improvement," 25–42)


Here there is no metaphoric contract, no organized connotative unity toward which the rhyme scheme, rhythmic pattern, and other devices are pointing. Instead there is the force of the thought that expresses itself in complex but balanced and repeated structures, and the conventional stanza lines seem to be rather like the "Churlish Proprieties . . . Bounds. . .[and] Divisions" which represent for him the "Dirty Devices of this World" (*CM* III.3) that he must unlearn. The thought, the idea of the poem, becomes the paramount concern, and whatever connotative process its expression may entail becomes absorbed by the repetitive, parallel units of thought as we see when the lines are rearranged:

To bring the Moisture of far distant Seas Into a *point*,
to make them present here, in *virtu,* not in *Bulk*;
One man to pleas with all the *Powers* of the Highest Sphere,
   from East,
   from West,
   from North and South,
  To bring the pleasing *Influence* of evry thing;
   Is far more Great
    Then to Creat them there Where now they stand;
His *Wisdom* more doth shine In that
his *Might* and *Goodness* more appear In recollecting;
He is more *Divine*
   In making evry Thing a Gift to one
Then in the Ports of all his Spacious *Throne*.

To see Traherne's lines arranged in this way makes their paralleling, repetitive form immediately apparent and demonstrates their lack of metaphor, and it suggests not only the answer to why he was a more successfully "poetic" writer of prose than of conventional verse but also the probability that had he been able to shape the conventional verse line into the form he needed to express his unitive vision he might have become one of poetry's great originals, as did Whitman. Gay Wilson Allen has made observations about Whitman and the backgrounds of his poetry that have remarkable appropriateness for Traherne as well:

But though this psychology ["of the expanding ego"] may be called the background or basic method of Whitman's poetic technique, the catalog itself . . . emerged only after he had found a verse structure appropriate for expressing his cosmic inspiration and democratic sentiment. Nowhere in the universe does he recognize caste or subordination. Everything is equally perfect and equally divine. He admits no supremes, or rather insists that "There can be any number of supremes."

The expression of such doctrines demands a form in which units are co-ordinate, distinctions eliminated, all flowing together in a synonymous or "democratic" structure. He needed a grammatical and rhetorical structure which would be cumulative in effect rather than logical or progressive.

Possibly, as many critics have believed, he found such a structure in the primitive rhythms of the King James Bible. . . . The structure of Hebraic poetry, even in English translation, is almost lacking in subordination.[9]

When Traherne wrote in prose, his natural sensitivity to rhythm, sound, and image guided him securely, and his work takes on all the qualities that Allen here attributes to Whitman. When Traherne wrote in poetry, the models of traditional versification that were available to him were, however, too strong to overturn, and that is why his poetry contains many isolated phrases and whole stanzas of considerable beauty and tightness of construction, but not as many fully integrated whole poems. It is also why Traherne's poetic practice is primarily symbolic and abstract rather than metaphoric and concrete and why he often seems to be arbitrary in his choice of words and unplanned or "open" in terms of structure. His poetry cannot be explained or justified simply by uncovering his mystical thought (for that thought is also fully expressed in his prose) nor by calling attention to his tendency to destroy, through abstractions and repetitions, the integrity of "limits and boundaries." Traherne was a mystic and both in prose and in poetry he did seek to demonstrate the falseness of the limiting illusion; but what must finally be explained is why there is so noticeable a difference between the level of mastery in such prose as meditation three of Century Three and the level of the best of the poetry, whichever poem we may wish to call his best. The explanation lies in the freedom Traherne felt to pursue in prose the repetitive forms that were natural to the expression of his vision. In poetry he was restricted by the conventional forms of verse that were the inheritance of his historical age.

### Traherne's Felicities

But all of this is not to deny that much of Traherne's poetry is admirable and effective, especially for the reader who can participate with Traherne in the excitement of contemplating highly abstract, metaphysical ideas. It is about the meaning of these for the soul in its quest for the ultimate perception of God that Traherne always writes—even when he seems to be interested in the concrete or the sensual experience. In "The Odour," for example, which exists in Philip's version alone, there is strong sensual imagery relating to the body, based upon the Song of Songs, but it is, characteristically, the spiritual meaning of any sense perception, its *use,* that is finally Traherne's real concern:

> Like Amber fair thy Fingers grow;
> With fragrant Hony-sucks thy Head is crown'd;
> Like Stars, thine Eys; thy Cheeks like Roses shew:
>             All are Delights profound.
> Talk with thy self; thy self enjoy and see:
> At once the Mirror and the Object be.
>
>             What's Cinnamon, compar'd to thee?
> Thy Body is than Cedars better far:
> Those Fruits and Flowers which in Fields I see,
>             With *Thine,* can not compare.
> Where ere thou movest, there the Scent I find
> Of fragrant Myrrh and Aloes left behind.
>
>             But what is Myrrh? What Cinnamon?
> What Aloes, Cassia, Spices, Hony, Wine?
> O sacred *Uses*! You to think upon
>             Than these I more incline.
> To see, taste, smell, observ; is to no End,
> If I *the Use* of each don't apprehend.
>
> ("The Odour," 49–66)

The poem as a whole is not quite equal to these stanzas, which do not seem marred by the conflict between Traherne's repetitive form and traditional verse conventions; but even here we are not allowed to dwell long on the sense detail and are asked instead to seek its spiritual meaning and to contemplate its intelligible idea.

Stanley Stewart has made analyses of several poems that exist only in the Burney manuscript and called attention to the interesting thought and beauties of such poems as "Shadows in the Water" and "On Leaping over the Moon."[10] These poems are admirable even though we cannot know precisely how much altered they are by Philip's editing, and they are an integral part of the progress of ideas as the Burney sequence unfolds from the vision of innocence through the soul's apostasy and its gradual recognition in maturity of what that vision is and means. But as an example of what poetic heights Traherne could rise to, it is well to choose a poem from the Dobell group wherein we know the lines can be trusted. An excellent illustrative poem is "The Rapture." It is brief and successful and in Traherne's best ecstatic style. It also invites comparison with the lyrics of William Blake. Traherne writes:

1

Sweet Infancy!
O fire of Heaven! O Sacred Light!
How Fair and Bright!
How Great am I,
Whom all the World doth magnifie!

2

O Heavenly Joy!
O Great and Sacred Blessedness,
Which I possess!
So great a Joy
Who did into my Armes convey!

3

From GOD abov
Being sent, the Heavens me enflame,
To prais his Name.
The Stars do move!
The Burning Sun doth shew his Love.

4

O how Divine
Am I! To all this Sacred Wealth,
This Life and Health,
Who raisd? Who mine
Did make the same? What Hand Divine!

("The Rapture," 1–20)

The short phrases that run throughout the poem celebrate the infant
vision and imitate the wonder felt at the splendor of the newly discovered world. Instead of seeking at once to explain or to grasp the Creation
with the categorizing function of the mind, the infant soul simply
"apprehends" or contemplates it in an act of pure admiration that asks
only what the source of it is: "So great a Joy / Who did into my Armes
convey!" The brightness, the wealth, and the splendor of the Creation
so fill the soul's attention that it is inflamed with the "fire of Heaven"
and magnified by its "Sacred Light" which is reflected in the natural

things of the world. The language here enhances a sense of the almost overwhelming richness of the vision, as if the soul is "burning" with its "blessedness," as the sun is burning in its demonstration of God's love. The connotations of these images work in harmony even though that harmony is based upon a broad and general sense of bright, sacred beauty. We see no objects clearly in their detail, but through the short phrases that mention those objects we are given a cumulative effect of similar associations or impressions without a connective logic between them. We have something like a series of snapshots of temporally disconnected but thematically similar things. Like the natural world to which the infant soul is responding, all of the separate things add up to one glorious meaning, but their source always remains the fundamental mystery of our existence: "To all this Sacred Wealth, / This Life and Health, / Who raisd? Who mine / Did make the same? What Hand Divine?"

Thus, as in Traherne's work generally, a surface simplicity, the perspective of a child's open wonder at the Creation, masks a profound insight into the mystery of Being and Existence, eternity and time, the many and the One. The individual soul (the many) is shown by the gloriousness of the universe, which it possesses and to which it also belongs, that it is "part of" the One that is its ultimate source:

> Sweet Infancy!
> O fire of Heaven! O Sacred Light!
> How Fair and Bright!
> How Great am I,
> Whom all the World doth magnifie!

And this combination of simplicity with deep mystery is achieved here through the ecstatic expostulations of a child who is filled with the splendor of the Creation and feels its secret meaning but does not connect things with each other in terms of temporal logic. In this brief lyric Traherne has expressed everything that is essential to his whole unitive vision, and the repetitive, paralleling structures (here appearing as short expostulations) work perfectly with the conventional rhyme scheme and line length partly because there is little connectedness between those objects that the infant sees. The poem is reminiscent of

Blake's "The Lamb" in its childlike questioning of the nature of experience, but if we look at only a stanza or two of Blake's poem, its stronger temporal logic, its clearer statement of the relationship of things in a sequential process, is immediately apparent:

Little Lamb who made thee?
Dost thou know who made thee?
Gave thee life & bid thee feed,
By the stream & o'er the mead;
Gave thee clothing of delight,
Softest clothing wooly bright;
Gave thee such a tender voice,
Making all the vales rejoice:
Little Lamb, who made thee
Dost thou know who made thee?[11]

We may perhaps prefer Blake's more fully connotative statement, but Traherne's innocent lyric, by virtue of the techniques we have seen throughout his work, moves us more directly and immediately into the mystery of Being itself. Traherne possesses in highest degree that ability to give us a direct experience of the infinite, eternal reality in which we exist, and when those repetitive devices that are natural to his prose are in harmony with the structures of lyric poetry—as they are in "The Rapture"—that experience is unequalled for ecstatic beauty and excitement. For many readers it may be that those moments of harmony are relatively rare, but it is at least clear that they are achieved by a blending of the regular verse line with an incantatory naming of the inexhaustible riches of the universe, placed (like exquisite jewels in their setting) forever in the infinite, eternal Mind of God. All of the devices of repetition that we have discovered Traherne working with in his most characteristic prose are, thus, also the most potent forces shaping his poetry, but, curiously, they are as much responsible for his failures, when they are in conflict with inherited poetic conventions, as they are responsible for his successes, when they are in harmony with the structures of lyric verse as he knew them. We have seen many other characteristics in Traherne's work, but this one quality, the direct sensation of eternity, can be traced like an unbroken thread through almost everything he wrote.

# Notes and References

*Chapter One*

1. See H. M. Margoliouth, ed., *Thomas Traherne: Centuries, Poems, and Thanksgivings,* 2 vols. (Oxford, 1958), 1:xxiii–xxxvii. Additional items of chronology and attribution can be found in several papers by Carol Marks, especially "Traherne's Church's Year-Book," *Papers of the Bibliographical Society of America* 60 (1966): 31–72; Anne Ridler, "Traherne: Some Wrong Attributions," *Review of English Studies* 18 (February 1967): 48–49; and [Richard] Lynn Sauls, "Traherne's Hand in the Credenhill Records," *The Library* 24 (1969): 50. For the reader's convenience, all references to biographical data which Margoliouth includes will be referred to his edition. Gladys Wade, *Thomas Traherne: A Critical Biography* (Princeton, 1944), is sometimes helpful although her speculative and sentimental approach to biographical "facts" is a serious flaw.

2. Margoliouth, 1: xxxvii.

3. *Athenae Oxonienses* (1691–92), in Margoliouth, 1: xxiii; and *Miscellanies* (1696), in Margoliouth, 1: xxviii.

4. From the Lambeth Palace Library MS. 998, in Margoliouth, 1: xxiv.

5. Margoliouth, 1: xxxvi.

6. As Sauls points out in his note on Traherne's signature in the Credenhill records, the parish register (which is complete from 1662 through the years Traherne could have been there) is signed by him for the first time in 1664. He signed it thereafter in 1665, 1667, and 1668. The Brasenose College Register also contains an interesting though equivocal note. Immediately after the record of his receiving the M.A. in November 1661 is written, "readm. 9 Dec." (Margoliouth, 1: xxiv). In view of this note and the fact that Traherne's hand does not appear in the Credenhill records until 1664, it is surprising that Margoliouth could say that Traherne "resided at Credenhill as rector from 1661–1669" (1: xxxvii). What evidence there is suggests, instead, a residency from 1664–1668/9.

7. Wade makes this speculation, which may have some merit, but she romanticizes Traherne's social position in order to present him as "an obscure Herefordshire rector" who was offered a "highly coveted. . . post" by the "eminent lawyer" and Lord Keeper, Sir Orlando Bridgeman. See Wade, p. 87.

8. See Wade, pp. 87, 112. Marks, in her edition (with George Guffey) of *Christian Ethicks* (Ithaca, 1968), says that Finch's wife "belonged to the Harvey family of Herefordshire, of which . . . Mrs. Hopton was a member" (p. xxviii, n. 43), but the articles in the *Dictionary of National Biography* for Susanna Hopton and Heneage Finch (the younger) claim that Mrs. Hopton's family was from Staffordshire and that Finch married an Elizabeth Harvey, sister of Daniel Harvey, a London merchant.

9. Dobell, in the introduction to his edition of the poems (reprinted in Wade's 1932 edition), helped draw a picture of Traherne as a simple and naturally happy child of God, a picture that has been difficult to alter: "The poet was, it is plain, one of those rare and enviable individuals in whom no jarring element is present, who come into the world as into their rightful inheritance, and whose life is a song of thankfulness for the happiness which they enjoy in it." In Gladys Wade, ed., *The Poetical Works of Thomas Traherne* (London, 1932; reprinted, New York, 1965), p. lvi. Wade, of course, echoes this in her biography, p. 3.

10. From the preface to the *Thanksgivings,* printed anonymously by Reverend Doctor Hicks as *A Serious and Pathetical Contemplation of the Mercies of God, in Several Most Devout and Sublime Thanksgivings for the Same* (London: Samuel Keble, 1699). In Margoliouth, 1: xxxii.

11. Margoliouth, 1: xxviii.

12. All references to *Centuries of Meditations,* unless otherwise noted, are from the Margoliouth edition and will be cited in the text by century and meditation number, as above.

13. Douglas Bush, *English Literature in the Earlier Seventeenth Century,* 2d ed. (New York: Oxford University Press, 1962), p. 158.

14. Marks, "Year-Book," pp. 71–72.

15. Quoted from *Major Poets of the Earlier Seventeenth Century,* Barbara Lewalski and Andrew Sabol, eds. (New York: The Odyssey Press, 1973).

16. For a valuable analysis of how the new Restoration Anglican writers and preachers were shaping the attitude toward reason, see Irene Simon, *Three Restoraton Divines: Barrow, South, Tillotson* (Paris: Société d'Edition Les Belles Lettres, 1967), esp. "Chapter Two: Anglican Rationalism in the Seventeenth Century."

17. Joseph Glanvill, *The Vanity of Dogmatizing: The Three 'Versions',* ed. Stephen Medcalf (Hove, Sussex: The Harvester Press, 1970) pp. 226–27.

18. Ibid., sig. A3r.

19. *The Works of that Eminent and Most Learned Prelate, Dr. Edward Stillingfleet,* 6 vols. (London: J. Hepstinstall, 1707–10), 5: A4v.

20. G. R. Cragg, *From Puritanism to the Age of Reason: A Study of Changes in Religious Thought Within the Church of England 1660 to 1700* (Cambridge: At the University Press, 1950), p. 34.

21. Helen C. White, Ruth C. Wallerstein, and Ricardo Quintana, eds., *Seventeenth-Century Verse and Prose,* 2 vols. (New York: Macmillan Company, 1952), 2:9.

22. Quoted by Cragg, p. 34.

23. South advises, for example, "That the *Voice* of Reason, in all the Dictates of *Natural Morality,* ought carefully to be attended to," and Tillotson asserts "that virtue and vice are not arbitrary things . . . there is a natural and immutable and eternal reason for that which we call goodness and virtue." In White et al., 2:196, 202.

24. C. S. Lewis, *The Discarded Image: An Introduction to Medieval and Renaissance Literature* (Cambridge: At the University Press, 1970), p. 157. Lewis is here quoting from Thomas Aquinas, in part.

25. See Robert Hoopes, *Right Reason in the English Renaissance* (Cambridge: Harvard University Press, 1962), pp. 21–22.

26. Cragg, pp. 63–64.

27. Ernst Cassirer, *The Platonic Renaissance in England,* trans. James P. Pettegrove (Austin: University of Texas Press, 1953), pp. 60–61.

28. Nathanael Culverwell, *An Elegant and Learned Discourse of the Light of Nature, with Severall Other Treatises* (London: John Rothwel, 1654), p. 5.

29. Benjamin Whichcote, *Moral and Religious Aphorisms,* Number 644, in *The Cambridge Platonists,* C. A. Patrides, ed. (Cambridge: Harvard University Press, 1970), p. 332. Hereafter cited as Patrides, *Platonists.*

30. Glanvill, p. 104.

31. Ibid., p. 105.

32. Henry More, *Enthusiasmus Triumphatus,* sec. 63, quoted by Aharon Lichtenstein, *Henry More: The Rational Theology of a Cambridge Platonist* (Cambridge: Harvard University Press, 1962), pp. 77–78.

33. Marks, "Thomas Traherne's Early Studies," p. 518.

34. See William T. Costello, *The Scholastic Curriculum at Early Seventeenth-Century Cambridge* (Cambridge: Harvard University Press, 1958) for an enlightening discussion of the part such scholastic practices played in the life of students at Cambridge (as well as Oxford) shortly before and into Traherne's time.

35. Barbara J. Shapiro, *John Wilkins, 1614–1672: An intellectual Biography* (Berkely: University of California Press, 1969), p. 123. The book is an excellent description of the lively state of scientific study at Wadham as

well as the whole of Oxford. See also Mark H. Curtis, *Oxford and Cambridge in Transition: 1558–1642* (Oxford: Clarendon Press, 1959), pp. 227–60.

36. Shapiro, p. 133.

37. Ibid., p. 129.

38. As Stanley Fish phrases it in a discussion of this issue in *Self-Consuming Artifacts: The Experience of Seventeenth-Century Literature* (Berkeley: University of California Press, 1972), p. 381.

39. Edward Fowler (1632–1714), an apologist for the Latitudinarians, provides an excellent example of how contemporary intellectuals understood what it was these men were thinking. In *The Principles and Practices of Certain Moderate Divines of the Church of England, (greatly mis-understood) Truly Represented and Defended* (London: Lodowick Lloyd, 1670), Fowler takes a position that is clearly an application of deductive reason to religion. Although his tone is much drier and more deistic than Traherne's, Fowler expresses Traherne's position that by the use of reason man can *"draw clear Inferences from evident Principles,"* that these "self-evident Principles of the Gospel" (p. 70) tell us that "the imitation of the Divine Nature, is the whole design of the Christian Religion" (p. 72), and that even though its genuine mysteries make it more than a merely "natural" religion, Christianity's reasonableness "makes it a Religion as easie to be practised by Mankinde as can be: for all the Duties, wherein consisteth the substance of it must have continued to oblige us, whether they were therein expressed or no" (p. 92).

40. All references to *Christian Ethicks* are from the edition by Marks and Guffey and will be cited in the text as *CE* followed by page number.

41. Patrides, *Platonists,* p. 17.

42. *Hermes Mercurius Trismegistus, His Divine Pymander . . . Together with his Second Book, Called Asclepius,* trans. John Everard (London: Thomas Brewster, 1657), p. 159.

43. John Everard, *Some Gospel Treasures Opened* (London: Rapha Harford, 1653), p. 14.

44. Ibid., p. 60.

45. Thomas Vaughan, *A Hermeticall Banquet, Drest by a Spagiricall Cook* (London: Andrew Crooke, 1652), sig. B1.

46. Thomas Taylor, *Meditations from the Creatures,* 3d ed. (London: John Bartlet, 1632), p. 23.

47. Francis King, "Thomas Traherne: Intellect and Felicity," *Restoration Literature: Critical Approaches,* (London, 1972), p. 141.

48. Ibid., pp. 140–41.

49. Louis Martz, *The Paradise Within* (New Haven, 1964), p. 48. His full statement is: "Thus by cogitating, assembling, various transistory

examples of the good, the mind in meditation draws toward an inward understanding of the good."

50. See, especially, A. L. Clements, *The Mystical Poetry of Thomas Traherne* (Cambridge, 1969) and Allison J. Sherrington, *Mystical Symbolism in the Poetry of Thomas Traherne* (St. Lucia, Australia, 1970).

51. See Stanley Stewart, *The Expanded Voice: The Art of Thomas Traherne* (San Marino, CA., 1970).

52. Patrides, *Platonists,* p. 36, n. 1, provides useful information concerning the origin of this well-known statement that God is a circle whose center is everywhere and whose circumference nowhere. He writes: "This famous affirmation has been traced (by E. Gilson . . .) to an anonymous work of the twelfth century, generally known as *Liber XXIV philosophorum* and attributed to 'Hermes' by Alan of Lille and others."

*Chapter Two*

1. Nicholas of Cusa, *The Vision of God* (1453), trans. Emma Gurney Salter (New York: E. P. Dutton, 1928), p. 12.

2. Stewart, *Expanded Voice,* pp. 70–71.

3. See Jackson I. Cope, "Seventeenth-Century Quaker Style," in *Seventeenth Century Prose: Modern Essays in Criticism,* ed. Stanley Fish (New York: Oxford University Press, 1971), p. 200.

4. Ibid., p. 204.

5. These three "motives" for Traherne's repetitive style have been suggested respectively by Stanley Stewart, Joan Webber in *The Eloquent "I"* (Madison, WI., 1968), and Arthur Clements.

6. Pico della Mirandola, "A Platonick Discourse Written . . . In explication of a Sonnet by Hieronimo Benivieni," in Thomas Stanley, *The History of Philosophy,* 2d ed. (London: T. Bassett, 1687), p. 198. Compare Paul Kristeller, *The Philosophy of Marsilio Ficino,* trans. Virginia Conant (New York: Columbia University Press, 1943; reprint ed., Gloucester, Mass: Peter Smith, 1964), p. 246, and Eugene Rice, *The Renaissance Idea of Wisdom* (Cambridge: Harvard University Press, 1958), p. 63.

7. John Norris, *The Theory of the Ideal or Intelligble World,* 2 vols. (London: S. Manship, 1701–04; facsimile ed., Hildesheim: Georg Olms Verlag, 1974), 1:9.

8. See the excellent introduction to the *Ethicks* by Marks, especially pp. xv–xxxvi. Because of the thoroughness of this introduction it has been possible to concentrate here upon analysis of Traherne's thought and style,

but for a description of the *Ethicks* in relation to its historical and contemporary backgrounds Marks is essential.

9. Glanvill, *Dogmatizing,* pp. 143–44.

10. Aquinas also places Repentance in the Theological Virtues.

11. See the *Summa Theologica,* II, I, Q. 57, Art. 4 and Q. 61, Art. 1.

12. Book 1, 1094b, 10, W. D. Ross, trans., Great Books of the Western World, vol. 9 (Chicago: Encyclopaedia Britannica, 1952), p. 339.

13. Vivian De Sola Pinto, *Peter Sterry: Platonist and Puritan: A Biographical and Critical Study with Passages Selected from his Writings* (Cambridge: At the University Press, 1934; reprint ed., New York: Greenwood Press, 1968), p. 90.

14. *Meister Eckhart: A Modern Translation,* ed. and trans. Raymond Blakney (New York: Harper Torchbooks, 1941), p. 209.

15. Cusa, pp. 48–49.

16. Both Edgar Wind, *Pagan Mysteries in the Renaissance,* new and enl. ed. (New York: Barnes and Noble, 1968), pp. 225, 239, and John Nelson, *Renaissance Theory of Love: The Context of Giordano Bruno's 'Eroici furori'* (New York: Columbia University Press, 1958), p. 256, n. 19, make this point.

17. Cusa, pp. 19, 117.

18. *The Philosophy of Love* (1535), trans. F. Friedeberg-Seeley and Jean H. Barnes with an introduction by Cecil Roth (London: Soncino Press, 1937), pp. 45–46.

19. Consider, also, the words of Meister Eckhart as quoted by Ananda K. Coomaraswamy, *Time and Eternity* (Ascona, Switzerland: Artibus Asiae, 1947), p. 124:

"to have all that has being and is lustily to be desired and brings delight; to have it simultaneously and partless. . . in the soul entire and that in God, revealed in its unveiled perfection, where first it burgeons forth and in the ground of its essence, and all there grasped where God grasps himself,—that is happiness."

20. Plotinus, *Ennead,* 2.9.16, says, for example: "To despise this Sphere, and the Gods within it or anything else that is lovely, is not the way to goodness." (*Plotinus: The Six Enneads,* trans., Stephen MacKenna and B. S. Page, Great Books of the Western World, vol. 17 (Chicago: Encyclopaedia Britannica, 1952), p. 76.

21. It must always be kept in mind that, in a sense, when Traherne speaks of many souls he is speaking in the language of "accommodation," or symbolically, for "there is no other approach to a knowledge of things divine than that of symbols." [Nicholas Cusanus, *Of Learned Ignorance,* trans. Germain Heron (New Haven: Yale University Press, 1954), p. 27.]

It is only the symbolic, "provisional" use of language, where statements are true in one way and untrue in another, that can express the proper understanding of the integral nature of both the essential (in essence) and the existential (in existence) planes. Traherne's basically metaphysical and esoteric mode of thinking assumes an identity of God and the soul on the essential plane (in fact *must* do so if God is pure Being—the Intelligible World), but of course also recognizes otherness on the plane of existence (the world of manifestation). As Cusa says, in another expression of the Intelligible World concept: "In it [the Absolute, or God] all the essences of things which have been or are still to be are always eternally in act its very essence; just as it is the essence of all, so is it all the essences; . . . it . . . is each of them and none of them in particular." (Cusanus, *Ignorance,* p. 35.) That the soul is "in essence" identical with God, then, in no way "edit[s] out the plural form of 'soul' in Traherne," as Richard Jordan claims in *The Temple of Eternity* (Port Washington, N.Y., 1972), p. 34.

22. Margaret Bottrall, "Traherne's Praise of the Creation," p. 130, writes: "The more we read Traherne, the more we must be struck by his passionate intellectuality. Not things, but thoughts of things are what he values." See also S. L. Bethell, *The Cultural Revolution of the Seventeenth Century* (New York: Roy Publishers, 1951), p. 157; and Itrat-Husain, *The Mystical Element in the Metaphysical Poets of the Seventeenth Century* (Edinburgh: Oliver and Boyd, 1948), p. 298.

23. Sir Thomas Browne, *Religio Medici,* ed. James Winney (Cambridge: At the University Press, 1963), pp. 15–16.

24. Cassirer, *Platonic,* p. 49, makes the point that the Cambridge Platonists held no value higher than contemplation.

25. Fish, *Artifacts,* p. 364.

26. Ibid., p. 371.

27. Ibid., pp. 49–50.

28. Ibid., p. 371.

29. Stewart, *Expanded Voice,* p. 210.

30. Fish, pp. 41–43.


*Chapter Three*

1. The *Six Days,* as it will usually be referred to for the sake of convenience, has been published in facsimile by George Robert Guffey, ed., *Thomas Traherne: Meditations on the Six Days of the Creation,* The Augustan Reprint Society, No. 119 (Los Angeles: University of California, 1966). All references are to this edition.

2. Wade, *Traherne,* p. 154.

3. "Traherne's debt to Puente's Meditations," *Philological Quarterly* 50 (1971): 163. See also, Catherine A. Owen, "The Authorship of the 'Meditations on the Six Days of Creation' and the 'Meditations and Devotions on the Life of Christ,'" *Modern Language Review* 56 (January 1961): 1–12, and Helen White, *The Metaphysical Poets* (New York: Macmillan, 1936).

4. Sauls, "Debt," p. 163.

5. Ibid., p. 169.

6. As Marks, "Year-Book," p. 31, describes it.

7. Sauls, *"Debt,"* p. 173.

8. Ibid., pp. 161, 162, 163.

9. "Year-Book," p. 35.

10. The manuscript of these meditations, which may be an early draft of the *Centuries,* came to light in 1964 and is to be published as the third volume in the Oxford edition of the works, but their publication has been much delayed, partly by the death of James Osborn, who discovered and was to edit them. For the first notice of their discovery see James Osborn, "A New Traherne Manuscript," *Times Literary Supplement,* October 8, 1964, p. 928.

11. Luis de la Puente, *Meditations upon the Mysteries of our Holie Faith, With the Practice of Mental Prayer Touching the Same,* 2 vols., trans. John Heigham (St. Omers: n.p., 1619), 1: 43.

12. Ibid., 1: 42.

13. Ibid.

14. Arnold Williams, *The Common Expositor: An Account of the Commentaries on Genesis, 1527–1633* (Chapel Hill: University of North Carolina Press, 1948), p. 259.

15. Puente, 2: 708.

16. See Sauls, "Debt," p. 164, n. 8.

17. Puente, 2: 708.

18. As Sauls, "Debt," p. 163, n. 7, points out.

19. Puente, 2: 752.

20. Ibid., 2: 760.

*Chapter Four*

1. Stewart, *Expanded Voice,* p. 97.

2. *Jerusalem and Albion: The Hebraic Factor in Seventeenth-Century Literature* (New York: Schocken Books 1964), p. 53.

3. For example, Joseph Hall, *Meditations and Vows, Divine and Moral* (1603), in *The Works of the Right Reverend Joseph Hall, D.D.,* 10 vols., new rev. and ed. Philip Wynter (Oxford: At the University Press, 1863), 7: 428,

and Daniel Featley, *Ancilla Pietatis: or, The Hand-Maid to Private Devotion* (London: N. Bourne, 1626), p. 18. Featley could be Traherne's immediate source, but the phrase was probably a commonplace.

4. As Ronald E. McFarland has also pointed out in "Thomas Traherne's *Thanksgivings* . . .," pp. 7–9. McFarland thinks because there is a "summary passage" (p. 7) in the Seventh Thanksgiving, "Thanksgivings for the Wisdom of his WORD," which mentions the subjects of previous Thanksgivings, that "Traherne originally intended it to end the sequence" (p. 7), but he neglects an even more obvious summary of the whole sequence at the beginning of Thanksgiving Eight. Thus, as I point out below, there is more reason to see Thanksgivings One through Eight than One through Seven as constituting a sequence. McFarland's thesis is that in the *Thanksgivings* Traherne "develops a theology of optimism through . . . a religious experience that centers around an active life in this world" and that this makes Traherne's thinking closer "to the Enlightenment than to his own century" (p. 3), but Traherne's theology has essentially nothing to do with "this world" insofar as such a phrase distinguishes a temporal from a nontemporal mode of experience, for even though Traherne understands the fact that experience takes place in a "temporal setting," he does not affirm that experience is necessarily "of this world." Experience takes place *in* the world, but Traherne insisted that it should be apprehended in its eternal, infinite meaning, which is not *of* the world in the sense that "active life in this world" would imply. That Traherne's thinking is optimistic and that this optimism is related to the Restoration and Enlightenment's general trust in man's ability to think things out for himself is true enough, but his thinking affirms the Creation because it perceives the Creation as ultimately spiritual, not the material thing that those who are "of the world" suppose it is. The *Thanksgivings* is, finally, no more optimistic than any other of Traherne's work, and to say that it is "devoted to the affirmation of man's condition in the temporal world" (p. 14) except as man is to understand that world spiritually (the *Centuries* and the *Ethicks* affirm man's condition also) seems either to be in error or to be making a distinction without a difference.

5. *The Poetry of Meditation: A Study in English Literature of the Seventeenth Century* (New Haven: Yale University Press, 1954), p. 38.

6. Puente, *Meditations,* 1: 16.

7. Martz, *Poetry,* p. 37.

8. Puente, 1: 3–4. Quoted by Martz, *Poetry,* pp. 34–35.

9. All quotations of the *Thanksgivings* are from the Margoliouth edition and will be referred to by line number.

10. See above, note 4.

11. "The Language of Vision: Traherne's Cataloguing Style," 94.

12. Ibid., p. 96.

13. *The Private Devotions of Lancelot Andrewes,* trans. F. E. Brightman (London: Methuen and Co., 1903; reprint ed., New York: Meridian Living Age Books, 1961), p. 47.

*Chapter Five*

1. Margoliouth, 1: xxxviii.

2. Marks, "Year-Book," pp. 60–61.

3. See Stillingfleet, "The Reformation Justified: Preached at Guild-Hall Chapel Septemb. 21. 1673," Sermon 13, in *Works,* 1:192. See note 19, Chapter 1, above.

4. *Roman Forgeries: Or a True Account of False Records Discovering the Impostures and Counterfeit Antiquities of the Church of Rome* (London: 1673). All references to *Forgeries* will be cited in the text as *RF* followed by page number.

5. This approach was given its most famous statement by Hooker, but it was already inherent in Bishop Jewel's methods of debate. See W. M. Southgate, *John Jewel and the Problem of Doctrinal Authority* (Cambridge: Harvard University Press, 1962), pp. 188–91.

6. This position concerning the primitive church was restated many times. Its popularity while Traherne was writing his polemic is attested by an anonymous pamphlet whose title plainly asserts the political implications of Romanism which worried Traherne and others in the Anglican establishment. See *The Religion of the Church of England, the Surest Establishment of the Royal Throne; With the Unreasonable Latitude which the Romanists allow in Point of Obedience to Princes* (London: Randal Taylor and John Williams, 1673), p. 5: "It may well be presumed that in those early dayes of Christianity Religion was in its greatest vigour, and men did not only *best* Know, but Practice what they were obliged to."

7. William Crashaw, *Romish Forgeries and Falsifications: Together with Catholike Restitutions* (London: Matthew Lownes, 1606), sig. E4v.

8. Thomas James, *A Treatise of the Corruption of Scripture, Councels, and Fathers by the Prelates, Pastors, and Pillars of the Church of Rome, for Maintenance of Popery and Irreligion,* in 5 parts (London: Matthew Lownes, 1612), 4:31.

9. See W. K. Jordan, *The Development of Religious Toleration in England;* vol. 1: *From the Beginning of the English Reformation to the Death of Elizabeth;* vol. 2: *From the Accession of James 1 to the Convention of the Long Parliament;* vol. 3: *From the Convention of the Long Parliament to the Restoration;* vol. 4: *Attainment of the Theory and Accomodations in Thought and Institutions;* 4 vols. (Cambridge: Harvard University Press, 1932–1940; reprint ed., Gloucester, Mass.: Peter Smith, 1965), 4:17–19.

10. Crashaw, sig. B4.
11. Crashaw, sigs. C3v and D1.
12. James, 4:9.
13. Ibid., 1: "Dedication."
14. Southgate, p. 132.
15. See above, note 6. Tillotson, Stillingfleet, and Barrow also speak in the same way about the early church.
16. Stewart, *Expanded Voice,* p. 35.
17. See H. Burn-Murdoch, *The Development of the Papacy* (London: Faber and Faber, 1954), pp. 217–18.
18. Ibid., p. 219.
19. Stewart, p. 29; cf. p. 34.

*Chapter Six*

1. See the indispensable study by Carol Marks Sicherman, "Traherne's Ficino Notebook," pp. 73–81. It is to this article that I am indebted for information about the content and dating of the "Ficino Notebook" and its relation to the *Centuries.*
2. Martz, *Paradise,* pp. 56–57.
3. Gerard H. Cox, III, "Traherne's *Centuries* . . .," p. 23.
4. Jordan, *Temple,* p. 72.
5. Ibid., p. 74.
6. Alexander Ross, *A Centurie of Divine Meditations Upon Predestination, and Its Adjuncts: Wherein are Shewed the Comfortable Uses of this Doctrine* (London: James Young, 1646). Ross's meditations are very short, spare statements of doctrinal points and could harldy have served as a serious model for Traherne.
7. Hall, *Art of Meditation,* in *Works,* 6:49. See note 3, Chapter 4, above.
8. Ibid.
9. Joseph Hall, *Meditations and Vows, Divine and Moral* (1605), in *Works,* 7:443.
10. Ronald E. McFarland, "From Ambiguity to Paradox: Thomas Traherne's 'Things,'" *Wascana Review* 9 (1974): 114–23, discusses the ambiguity that surrounds Traherne's frequent use of *Thing*[*s*] in the poetry, where he sometimes means temporal objects and sometimes "thoughts." McFarland's conclusion is interesting, and it may be that *thing* has a special significance for understanding Traherne's thought, but the ambiguity in his use of the word is not unique; it is consistent with the ambiguities involved in Traherne's use of such other important words as *soul, mind, image,* and *self,* for they all have the same double nature—both finite and infinite—that he sees everywhere.

11. *The Bible as Literature* (New York, 1906), p. 107, quoted by Gay Wilson Allen, *Walt Whitman Handbook* (New York: Hendricks House, 1946), p. 389.

12. Allen, p. 402.

*Chapter Seven*

1. Osborn, "Manuscript," p. 928.

2. Ibid.

3. Martz, *Paradise,* p. 208.

4. See Osborn, p. 928.

5. Sharon C. Seelig, "The Origins of Ecstasy: Traherne's 'Select Meditations,'" pp. 419–31, has discussed the character of the "Select Meditations" and concluded that in this earlier work Traherne is generally more conservative, more involved with worldly affairs, and less optimistic than in the *Centuries.* She concentrates more than I upon the picture that one gets of Traherne the man and Christian, but her words are, I believe, exactly right and her study the most valuable one at present available. She writes (p. 420): "The persona who emerges is, in comparison to that of *Centuries,* a more traditional, conservative Christian, one more deeply involved in the affairs of the nation and the community, more closely allied to the established Church, more attentive to its ceremonies, doctrines, and benefits."

*Chapter Eight*

1. Clements, *Mystical Poetry,* p. 5.

2. See Sherrington, *Symbolism.*

3. Only the edition of the poems by Gladys Wade (1932)—which unfortunately does not preserve Thomas's version of individual poems where possible—prints both sequences in full as distinct groups. Margoliouth alters the order of both sequences in order to facilitate comparison between Thomas's and Philip's versions, and Anne Ridler, ed., *Thomas Traherne: Poems, Centuries and Three Thanksgivings* (London, 1966), prints the whole Dobell sequence in its order but only those poems of the Burney sequence that are *not* also included in Dobell. Because it makes at least the whole Dobell group available in its proper order, then, and corrects some errors in Margoliouth's edition, all citations of the poems are from the Ridler edition.

4. Clements, p. 59.

5. See Stewart, *Expanded Voice,* p. 185.

6. Allen, *Whitman,* p. 387.

7. Kenneth Burke, *Counter-Statement* (Los Altos: Hermes Publications, 1953), p. 125.

8. Ibid., p. 126.

9. Allen, *Whitman*, pp. 387–88.

10. Stewart, *Expanded Voice*, pp. 145–55.

11. Quoted from *Songs of Innocence and of Experience Shewing the Two Contrary States of the Human Soul,* A Reproduction of William Blake's Illuminated Book with Introduction and Commentary by Sir Geoffrey Keynes (Paris: Trianon Press, 1967; reprint ed., London: Oxford University Press, 1970), Plate 8.

# Selected Bibliography

**Primary Sources**

1. Published Works

*Christian Ethicks.* Edited by Carol L. Marks and George R. Guffey. Ithaca: Cornell University Press, 1968.

*Meditations on the Six Days of the Creation.* Edited with introduction by George R. Guffey. Augustan Reprint Society, No. 119. Los Angeles: Clark Memorial Library, 1966.

*The Poetical Works of Thomas Traherne.* Edited by Gladys Wade. London: P.J. and A.E. Dobell, 1932; reprint ed., New York: Cooper Square Publishers, 1965.

*Roman Forgeries, Or a True Account of False Records Discovering the Impostures and Counterfeit Antiquities of the Church of Rome.* By a Faithful Son of the Church of England. London: S. and B. Griffin for Jonathan Edwin, 1673.

*Thomas Traherne: Centuries, Poems, and Thanksgivings.* Edited by H. M. Margoliouth. 2 vols. Oxford: Clarendon Press, 1958.

*Thomas Traherne: Poems, Centuries, and Three Thanksgivings.* Edited by Ann Ridler, London: Oxford University Press, 1966.

2. Unpublished Manuscripts

"Early Notebook." (Bodleian Library, Oxford, MS. Lat. misc. f. 45)

"Church's Year Book." (Bodleian Library, Oxford, MS. Eng. th. e. 51)

"Commonplace Book." (Bodleian Library, Oxford, MS. Eng. poet. c. 42)

"Ficino Notebook." (British Museum, London, MS. Burney 126)

"Select Meditations." (Osborn Collecton, Beinecke Library. Yale)

**Secondary Sources**

1. Biographical and Critical Studies

Clements, A. L. *The Mystical Poetry of Thomas Traherne.* Cambridge: Harvard University Press, 1969. A fine study of the Dobell manuscript poems—their arrangement and language—in the light of the contemplative tradition.

Jordan, Richard Douglas. *The Temple of Eternity: Thomas Traherne's Philosophy of Time.* Port Washington, N. Y.: Kennikat Press, 1972. A worthwhile study of Traherne's concept of "eternity-time," though sometimes making distinctions without differences. Discusses the *Centuries* as patterned upon the Four Estates of man.

Salter, K. W. *Thomas Traherne: Mystic and Poet.* London: Edward Arnold, 1964. An attempt to analyze Traherne's spiritual life with some discussions of his ideas and poetic imagery.

Sherrington, Alison J. *Mystical Symbolism in the Poetry of Thomas Traherne.* St. Lucia, Australia: University of Queensland Press, 1970. An insightful analysis of Traherne's poetic imagery, demonstrating his essentially symbolic technique.

Stewart, Stanley. *The Expanded Voice: The Art of Thomas Traherne.* San Marino, Calif.: Huntington Library, 1970. A very useful discussion of Traherne's characteristic blurring of temporal categories and distinctions through his "rhetoric of erosion." Treats all the works plus manuscripts and proposes a new grouping of the Burney poems by removing all of the Dobell poems from it.

Wade, Gladys. *Thomas Traherne: A Critical Biography.* Princeton: Princeton University Press, 1944. The earliest biography and general study, marred by certain liberties with biographical evidence and an attempt to see into Traherne's soul, but still an important book with valuable information and insights.


2. Bibliographical Studies

Clements, A. L. "Thomas Traherne: A Chronological Bibliography." *Library Chronicle* 35 (1969): 36–51. Nearly complete through 1967.

———. "Addenda to 'Thomas Traherne: A Chronological Bibliography.'" *Library Chronicle* 42, No. 2 (1978): 138–45.

Dees, Jerome S. "Recent Studies in Traherne." *English Literary Renaissance* 4 (1974): 189–96. Succinct and useful, partially annotated bibliography of recent work to 1972.

Guffey, George Robert, ed. *A Concordance to the Poetry of Thomas Traherne.* Berkeley: University of California Press, 1974.

Marks, Carol L. "Thomas Traherne's Commonplace Book." *Papers of the Bibliographical Society of America* 58 (1964): 458–65. A close and valuable examination of Traherne's notes used extensively in the preparation of *Christian Ethicks*.

———. "Thomas Traherne's Early Studies." *Papers of the Bibliographical Society of America* 62 (1968): 511–36. A very important study of Traherne's earliest notebook, providing information about his reading while a student at Oxford.

———. "Traherne's Church Year-Book." *Papers of the Bibliographical Society of America* 60 (1966): 31–72. Indispensable study of a manuscript that provides links between several works and helps date *Roman Forgeries* as a product of the early 1670s not an earlier B.D. thesis as was supposed by Margoliouth.

Osborn, James M. "A New Traherne Manuscript." [London] *Times Literary Supplement,* 8 October 1964, p. 928. A brief announcement and description of the "Select Meditations."

Sauls, [Richard] Lynn. "Traherne's Debt to Puente's *Meditations.*" *Philological Quarterly* 50 (April 1971): 161–74. Describes significant discovery of Traherne's dependence upon Puente's work for the *Meditations on the Six Days of the Creation.*

Sicherman, Carol Marks. "Traherne's Ficino Notebook." *Papers of the Bibliographical Society of America* 63 (1969): 73–81. Important description of Traherne's studies in Renaissance Platonism in late 1660s.

3. Shorter Critical Studies

Bottrall, Margaret. "Traherne's Praise of Creation." *Critical Quarterly* 1 (Summer 1959): 126–33. Studies Traherne's spiritual imagination and explains his preference for thoughts over things.

Colie, Rosalie L. "Thomas Traherne and the Infinite: The Ethical Compromise." *Huntington Library Quarterly* 21 (November 1957): 69–82. A clear explanation of some of Traherne's most important ideas, emphasizing his insistence upon knowledge of the infinite as the means of salvation.

Cox, Gerard H., III. "Traherne's *Centuries*: A Platonic Devotion of 'Divine Philosophy.'" *Modern Philology* 69 (August 1971): 10–24. Sees the structure of the *Centuries* in Traherne's Platonic principles, and suggests an order based upon God's laws, works, and the self, concluding that the work is "an interesting failure."

Day, Malcolm M. " 'Naked Truth' and the Language of Thomas Traherne." *Studies in Philology* 68 (July 1971): 305–25. Discusses Traherne's use of abstraction and paradox as a means of bringing his reader to a perception of God.

———. "Traherne and the Doctrine of Pre-existence." *Studies in Philology* 65 (January 1968): 81–97. Argues that Traherne's mystical view includes a doctrine of the pre-existence of the impersonal, infinite-eternal soul.

Goldknopf, David. "The Disintegration of Symbol in a Meditative Poet."
   *College English* 30 (October 1968): 48–59. Discusses the problem of
   poetic imagery in Traherne's Neoplatonic perspective, which inher-
   ently disparages the senses.
Grant, Patrick. *The Transformation of Sin: Studies in Donne, Herbert, Vaughan,
   and Traherne.* Montreal: McGill-Queens University Press, 1974. An
   excellent study of Traherne's work against the contrast between an
   Augustinian "guilt" and an "enlightenment" culture. Sees Traherne in
   the light of the pre-Nicene St. Irenaeus's theology.
Jennings, Elizabeth. "The Accessible Art: A Study of Thomas Traherne's
   *Centuries of Meditations." Twentieth Century* 167 (February 1960): 140–
   51. The *Centuries* as an example of "the art of sharing."
King, Francis. "Thomas Traherne: Intellect and Felicity." In *Restoration
   Literature: Critical Approaches,* pp. 121–43. Edited by Harold Love.
   London: Methuen, 1972. Correctly sees that Traherne writes from the
   perspective of "realization" rather than search, but regards this perspec-
   tive as facilely adopted by Traherne.
Leishman, James Blair. *The Metaphysical Poets: Donne, Herbert, Vaughan,
   Traherne.* Oxford: Clarendon Press, 1934. A good early study of
   Traherne's place in the metaphysical poetic tradition.
McFarland, Ronald E. "From Ambiguity to Paradox: Thomas Traherne's
   'Things.'" *Wascana Review* 9 (1974): 114–23. Provides insight into
   Traherne's use of a "neutral" word to suggest an important point of
   philosophical discrimination.
———. "Thomas Traherne's *Thanksgivings* and the Theology of Optimism." *Enlightenment Essays* 4, No. 2 (Spring 1973): 3–14. An
   interesting study that points out the sequential nature of the *Thanksgivings* but claims a special importance of the work for Traherne's optimistic viewpoint.
Marks, Carol L. "Thomas Traherne and Cambridge Platonism." *Publications
   of the Modern Language Association* 81 (December 1966): 521–34. The
   best short analysis of the relationship of Traherne's thought to the ideas
   of the Cambridge Platonists.
———. "Thomas Traherne and Hermes Trismegistus." *Renaissance News* 19
   (1966): 118–31. Discusses Traherne's fascination with the philosophy of
   Hermes, arguing that Hermes provided affirmation of Traherne's own
   thinking.
Martz, Louis L. *The Paradise Within: Studies in Vaughan, Traherne, and
   Milton.* New Haven: Yale University Press, 1964. An important study
   of the *Centuries* in the Augustinian-Bonaventuran tradition of meditation. Sensitive and illuminating, although the thesis is somewhat
   misleading.

Ridlon, Harold G. "The Function of the 'Infant-Ey' in Traherne's Poetry." *Studies in Philology* 61 (1964): 627–39. Traherne's concept of infancy and childhood as a key to his theme of man's relation to God and the world.

Sandbank, S. "Thomas Traherne on the Place of Man in the Universe." In *Studies in English Language and Literature,* edited by Alice Shalvi and A. A. Mendilow, pp. 121–36. *Scripta Hierosolymitana: Publications of the Hebrew University,* vol. 17. Jerusalem: Magnes Press, 1966. One of the most intelligent and perceptive analyses of Traherne's efforts to "spiritualize" everything and affirm the dignity of man.

Seelig, Sharon C. "The Origins of Ecstasy: Traherne's 'Select Meditations.'" *English Literary Renaissance* 9 (1979): 419–31. A valuable commentary upon the still unpublished and unstudied meditations found by Osborn.

Selkin, Carl M. "The Language of Vision: Traherne's Cataloguing Style." *English Literary Renaissance* 6 (1976): 92–104. An analysis of Traherne's use of catalogues. Suggests that catalogues are a unitive, nonlinear language directly expressing a "deep level" vision of the oneness of all in God.

Trimpey, John E. "An Analysis of Traherne's 'Thoughts I.'" *Studies in Philology* 68 (1971): 88–104. Interesting discussion of Traherne's intellectual, "logical" mysticism by an examination of his assertions in one of the poems.

Uphaus, Robert. "Thomas Traherne: Perception as Process." *University of Windsor Review* 3 (Spring 1968): 19–27. Discusses the difference between "bare perception" and "apprehension" in Traherne's philosophy of apostasy and redemption.

Wallace, John Malcolm. "Thomas Traherne and the Structure of Meditation." *English Literary History* 25 (June 1958): 78–89. Claims that the Dobell sequence constitutes a complete five-part Ignatian meditation.

Webber, Joan. *The Eloquent "I": Style and Self in SeventeenthCentury Prose.* Madison: University of Wisconsin Press, 1968. Contains a valuable chapter on Traherne's merging of self and audience into a spiritual community through a typical use of rhetorical patterns.

Williams, Melvin G. "Thomas Traherne: Center of God's Wealth." *Cithara* 3 (1963): 32–40. Discusses Traherne's presumed self-centered Christianity.

# Index